Confessions of a College Freshman

By

Zach Arrington

RIVER
OAK
PUBLISHING

Confessions of a College Freshman:
A Survival Guide for Dorm Life, Biology Lab, the Cafeteria,
and Other First-Year Adventures
ISBN 1-58919-660-0
Copyright © 2001 by Zach Arrington

Published by RiverOak Publishing
P.O. Box 700143
Tulsa, Oklahoma 74170-0143

Excerpt titled *Girls Just Wanna Have Fun* copyright © 2001
by Kristen G. Green.

DEDICATION

To Andrew, a randomly chosen guy
on my hall. And to my mother,
without whom I would not have
half of my chromosomes.

ACKNOWLEDGMENTS

Special thanks to Don and Marie
Fitzgerald, my loving grandparents.
Without your generous support it would
have been impossible for me to
fulfill this dream. I love you.

Table of Contents:

Prologue
College? What?

If I were to believe what I see in the movies, I would tell you
that everyone in college is insanely beautiful all of the time,
except for the crazy people, who are hilarious all of the time.
Everyone uses "God" as a four-letter word—which it obviously
is not. Half of the people in college are constantly sleeping
with the other half, and the average beer consumption rate is
4.4 gallons per head, per night. Oh, and whenever a small,
run-down college with 800 people plays football against the
80,000 student state college, the small run-down college
will always win.

However, based on my one year of experience, college life
is not like that.

Anyway, the point is: Hi. My name is Zach, and for the rest of
this book I'll be taking you on a brief tour of my life. The
reason for this tour is I think most kids (or "young people"
as the preferred term seems to be) haven't the foggiest idea
of what to expect when they take flight from their nests and
head for college.

As I write this prologue, I'm about two months away from packing my bags for the final time, and "college" is still some abstract idea that doesn't seem to have a practical place in real life. Or rather it does but, like quantum physics, I don't know how it works. So, I hope as I relate my trials and triumphs, you can read and learn, call me when you make the same mistakes, so we can laugh and cry with each other, and I can hang up and wonder *Who was that?*

A brief autobiography: I was born on January 28, 1981 to my parents, Jack and Lael. I live in a small town (Tomball) twenty minutes away from a really big town (Houston). I play guitar and piano by ear. I love music. I write music, sing music, listen to music, study music. There's really not a whole lot more you can do with music, but if there were, I'd do it. If music were a fruit, I'd eat it. I trusted Christ at age four, and now I play guitar for my church youth group. That said, my favorite music was made in the late '60s and '70s by the Beatles and Led Zeppelin.

The thing I love even more than music is performing. Maybe it's because I have some kind of attention-dependency gene. Whatever the case, I'm happiest when I'm on stage. That's where I've always felt I belong. I'm sure when I was an infant I would throw up all over myself just so people would look at me. Following that logic, it seems only natural that I am now a theater performance major at Baylor University.

In four years of high school I attained varsity status in drama, basketball, and choir—without getting a letter jacket. I'm still trying to figure out how I managed that. I delivered the televised morning announcements with great flare and emceed many gala campus events like the Senior Girls' Powder Puff Football Game, the Cougar Charm's Drill Team Spring Extravaganza, and the Mr. Debonair Pageant, at which I succeeded in helping my best friend, Spencer, win. I had the high school world at my feet.

But, how ridiculous. Just about the time we start getting used to high school, they see fit to graduate us. During the last two or three weeks of my high school career I kind of figured out what I was doing. However, by that time I realized it was a little late to make much difference, so I went back to doing things the way I did them before I figured out what I was doing—only more so. Some people call this "senioritis." I call it seeing the light at the end of the tunnel.

Spencer was a little uncomfortable about leaving home for college. Not I. My house seemed like it was getting smaller every day. And although I love my parents to death, their endless barrage of tasks and requests was beginning to wear thin.

So, for the rest of this book, sit back, relax, don't fall asleep, and step into the shoes of a tall, college-bound 18-year-old who didn't really have a clue what was going on—but still managed to survive that first momentous year. Oh, by the way, at the end of this book, there's a 240-question exam with five essays. If you fail, you have to go back and read the book again. Just kidding—that's just a little college humor.

Time Management, Auto Theft, and General Naughtiness

It was a bright and sunny day when my family and I closed the last car door and began the treacherous (well, almost treacherous) journey west, into the unknown. The open road lay before us, and the uncharted possibilities began to take form. I almost shed a tear as I saw our little hometown fade into the distance behind us as the wheels of the car carried us relentlessly on our way to Baylor University. Everything I had ever known and loved was still in that little town that Tuesday afternoon: all my friends and memories, my youth group, my first bike. I was leaving them all behind to face a new challenge. But I was coming back in two days, since we were only going for freshman orientation.

You may wonder why this book does not start with the traditional "chapter 1." This, being a book about my college experience, should begin with my leaving for college. The place where the story starts is generally acknowledged to be "chapter 1." Since the real story hasn't started to take place yet, this chapter really can't be called, in all honesty, "chapter 1." So, the title "chapter 0" denotes that chronologically this chapter takes place before the events of . . . basically if you don't get it at this point, just admit to yourself that you don't get it and keep reading.

It's a two and one-half hour drive from Waco to our home. This, I think, is an optimal distance because it allows you, if you so desire, to return home on the weekends for money and laundry. However, it is too far away from home for your parents to make frequent and unannounced visits. This gives you the best of both worlds: privacy and dependency.

I passed the drive by reading some books that I have already completely forgotten. (Whether or not this is a bad omen, I don't know.) We arrived in Waco directly ahead of a huge thunderstorm that passed over us without so much as a drop of rain. This really upset me because I love rain.

Like most college-bound eighteen-year-olds, I love spending the night in a single hotel room with just two undersized beds and both my parents. My father's snores sound like a man with a chainsaw trying to down a giant Sequoia. My mother throws things in an effort to shut him up. I am sleeping on the floor with my head in the bathroom and my feet underneath the television. The next day I feel immensely rested and ready to tackle anything that college has to throw at me. Yeah right.

Orientation, or so they call it, consists mainly of sitting in a room and listening to people talk about various aspects of campus life. There are people from the registration office, people from the student life offices, people who are in charge of chapel, the ROTC guy, and several others giving their two cents about how to succeed at college life. "Keep your nose out of sex and booze and dope," they say. "We don't want to hear that you're being naughty. We have enough people locked up in the bell tower as it is."

A representative from campus security took the mike for about an hour (no kidding) and gave a very moving and eloquent speech on safety procedures at college. He launched into the subject of transportation on campus, starting first with the campus speed limit—twenty miles an hour. Yeah, right. He made sure we all were very aware of this fact before we left. He also said if you're planning on bringing a bike to school, those wimpy quarter-inch locks aren't going to cut it. He suggests getting a "U-lock," which is a massive lock shaped (I'll bet you can guess) like a "U." Also, he gave some common-sense tips, such as if you're bringing your Dodge Viper or Ferrari, please lock the doors. They've had bad experiences with people leaving their windows down and their wallets on the console.

One of the main topics everyone brought up was "time management." This is one of those mystical concepts you hear about in high school, but you aren't sure if it is a true thing or just another urban legend. The people at orientation made sure all doubts were dispelled. Here was time management in all of its splendor. We were advised on the use of calendars, watches, alarm clocks, schedules, study techniques, and even counselors to make sure we were keeping on top of everything. Time management, we were told, is the savior of our college GPAs.

Up to this point, the only time management advice I had received was, "Early morning might be a good time to do your Bible study." I also had to have my dates home by midnight. I was more or less used to just having homework float in (or out of) my schedule somewhere. But here I am expected to be "self-motivated" and "proactive." I previously thought you had to get a prescription for these kinds of things. So, I don't really know how I'm going to do at all this, but since this is only chapter 0, I still have a little time to figure it out.

When not talking about time management (dun-dun-dun-DUN), the presenters commented on the campus or their particular department. As usual during a lecture,

I took notes while the people were speaking. Here are some excerpts:

Baylor Registration (yeah!)

- The worst part about going to college is there are too many people here I don't know. I guess it's not their fault, really. They've just never been presented with the opportunity of meeting me.

- This man is wearing a purple shirt, and his hair sticks out to the side. Personally I abhor that shirt.

- I never knew fall registration was as exciting as this lady seems to think it is. I think she's some kind of marionette—I can vaguely make out strings hanging from the ceiling.

- Help! Help! My attention span is wearing thin!

- Blah blah blah blah blah blah information information information information blah blah blah blah blah.

- I'll bet come the first day of school I'll wish I had actually written the information out, instead of "blah blah blah information."

The next part of orientation was a little different. Like cattle, the adults were herded into one room, mooing about how nice the campus was and how they were sure that their children would be happy here. The children were herded into another room, mooing about members of the opposite sex. I have no idea what happened to the adults, but here is the children's story:

We arrived, all 200 of us, in a very plush "reading room" complete with chairs that looked like thrones, gothic fireplaces, and intricate woodwork. It was very posh. Being one of the first to arrive in the room, I picked the poshest chair I could find, and sank into it. I don't think I have ever been more comfortable in all my life. However, no sooner had I done that than the guy who was in charge of this activity said, "All right, now everybody find a partner! You have one minute!" This upset me greatly because as I looked up from the perfect bliss of that chair, I saw nothing around me but strange faces already getting partners.

I knew as soon as I got out of that chair to find a partner, some seat-greedy fellow was going to steal it. Faced with imminent uncomfortableness, I innovated. I happened to have a pen and paper handy. I drew a stick man on the pad, and underneath him I wrote the words: "Herman! (my partner)." As it turned out, I had to play a game with Herman that involved asking each other questions about campus life. The whole thing was organized as a competition against other groups. We lost.

The next day, I registered for classes, which all in all was pretty painless. We had to do some mixing and matching, but I got pretty much everything I wanted. The only problem was, because of my major I was going to wind up attending classes from 9:00 to 5:00. (Except for Tuesdays and Thursdays, when I would be required to be there at 8:30 in the morning!) I shall keep you updated as to how that works out.

So, all said and done, orientation was a mostly beneficial experience. It's the first official college thing you do, but you don't really have to worry about making first impressions, and you can kind of get a feel for what the other people in your class are going to be like. Seeing the campus is also very important, as this is going to be the backdrop for the next four years of your life. Obviously, orientation isn't bundles and bundles of fun, but you do learn about time management, and except for the bell tower, it's not unpleasant.

Chapter One

Strangers in a Strange Land

College is like a box of chocolates;
it makes you gain weight.

The day I never thought would come finally came. Or rather, I knew it would come, but kind of like the Rapture, I had never really planned on it happening. I don't think we ever really expect one day to wake up and say, "Oh my, the Rapture took place. Isn't this wonderful?" It's just one of those things that's always off in the distance. It's going to happen. There's no getting around it, but it just doesn't concern us right now. I never expected to wake up one morning and actually say, "Well, I've got to pack, I'm going to college today." Just a year ago, it would have been just as reasonable for someone to say to me, "All right, pack up everything you own! You're going to Jupiter today!"

The entire packing process ate up three whole days. I don't think there's a word in the English language that expresses the feeling you get when you pack everything you've ever owned into a car for the first time. You're sitting out in your driveway on a hot summer day, looking at your car. It's filled with junk to the point that you have a little six-inch square on your windshield you can look out of to drive. You look inside that car and think to yourself, "Hey, I got that basketball when I was seven years old." When you start thinking like that, you remember all the great memories you have of your home, and suddenly you wonder if you really want to leave. This shocks you, because 48 hours ago the only thing you wanted to do was get far, far away from your house and never look back.

Note to Reader:

At this point, your mother is going to go stark-raving looney. This might be a little unsettling at first, but remember this will be the first time she hasn't had to cook dinner for you in nearly two decades. Such severe changes in routine are almost always psychologically damaging.

In the course of three days, my parents and I totally rearranged all the furniture in my room, took the contents of an entire closet, an entire dresser, and along with a computer, packed them all into the rear and backseat of my 1990 Isuzu Trooper, then moved them two and one-half hours away, and unpacked them all. That done, the computer decided this was the perfect time to malfunction. I won't go into great detail about that episode. Let's just say given the right circumstances, computers respond very well to savage yells and heavy blows with metal objects.

It lies in wait for you.

Another problem presented by moving into a dorm room is this: How to get all the stuff that fit very well in a medium-to-large room into a four and one-half square feet space. (You think I'm kidding?) I was placed, by the Lords of Baylor, into a three-person room. A three-person room is very similar to a two-person room. In fact, the only thing that distinguishes a three-person room from a two-person room is it contains an extra person. So, take the same four-and-one-half square feet space you used to have to divide by two, and now divide it by three. That's how much space you have to store yourself and everything you call yours. (See Appendix A for relatively helpful hints about how to accomplish this.)

The first night in my dorm, I slept on top of my CD case. Let me explain: Finding nowhere else to put my CD case, and determining that it does, in fact, make for a somewhat comfortable footrest, I have been sleeping on it consistently since my arrival.

The dorms opened on a Friday, but classes didn't start until the next Wednesday. This gave me the better part of five days to wander aimlessly about the campus and wonder what in the wide world of sports I was supposed to be doing. Actually, this process can be quite exciting because any given person you meet on the street is wandering around just as aimlessly as you are. By about the fifth day you are part of a great wandering mob of people you don't really know, but it's better than wandering aimlessly alone.

One of the main things that struck me while wandering aimlessly was the sheer volume of people running around on this campus. In high school, you have a limited stock of people. In my case, about 2,000 people. By the time you're a senior, you know the face of almost everyone in your class, as well as all the "important people" in the other grades. Here, there is a vast sea of people. You can never hope to get to know all of them without severe social burnout. The best you can hope for is to pick out the ones who look like the kind of people you'd get along with, then get to know them.

A helpful upperclassman explained it to me as what I have come to call "the clean slate factor." Not only do you know less than 1 percent of the total people on campus, but the chances are, unless you do something creative like pelting people with water balloons from the top of the bell tower, most of them will never know you. The "popular crowd" is forever done away with. Whatever reputation you had in high school stays there.

Many people find this very liberating. I've heard many stories about high school "wallflowers" opening up and becoming college class presidents or something. However, people like me, who were pretty happy with the social scene in high school, can find it rather exasperating to find themselves starting over again. I mean, I know NO ONE here. Both of my roommates had the foresight to bring roughly half of their high school with them. So, they're out every night having a jolly old time with people they know and love, leaving me to my own resources.

However, I am not totally defenseless—mostly defenseless, yes—totally defenseless, no. About the second night, I decided it was high time to stop wallowing in self-pity. I grabbed my guitar, and found the most inviting tuft of grass available. Now it just so happened that this very inviting tuft of grass was growing just outside the largest girls' dorm on campus. Suddenly I found myself in very desirable company.

My two cents' worth of advice for those of you just about to step foot on a college campus: If there is ever a time in your life you just absolutely let it fly and go insane, let it be the first week of college. Don't get me wrong. Be conscious of what you're doing, and be very wary not to compromise your morals (and if you didn't have any in high school, you'd better get some in a hurry before things really get messed up for you), just let loose. Every social inhibition you have, be it bashfulness or an aversion to making a fool of yourself, give it a vacation for a week. After that you can retreat to your little comfort zone, but you'll have friends and connections that will benefit you for the rest of your college career, if not your life.

That said, I want to put a little disclaimer in this book. Even though I am giving you tips, offering you advice, and providing you a guide through your first year of college, please don't mistake this as evidence I know what I am doing. I don't want to make it seem I'm some sort of college demigod who knows all and sees all—and who is giving you foolproof guidelines that will turn you into an overnight success. I'm just trying to make college real for you, and put a more friendly face on the frightening specter of moving away. Right now I'm just as lost as you are, or will be, or whatever. The point is: I'm just this guy, you know?

Another thing I noticed on campus is how old everyone is. It's actually kind of intimidating. As a high school senior, half of the freshmen class look as if they just put away their "My Little Pony" toys. Then, suddenly, you're thrown into the mix with people who buy beer. *Legally!* You're going to the same school with guys who are so hairy they look like walking shrubs, and girls who look like they should be going to pick up their kids from soccer practice.

Of course, the funny thing is that if you look in the mirror you will discover you don't quite look like you just put away your My Little Pony either. This, I have observed, is a trend that will stick with you for the rest of your life. You always think you're younger than you are. Who knows? Maybe the next time I look in the mirror I *will* be picking up the kids.

You know what? I don't even want to deal with that right now, and I don't think you should either. Just forget everything I said in the previous paragraph. The only reason I'm going to leave it in is so that when I'm forty I can read it and see how right I was. I'm just not going to think about it now. Shoot, we're teens. We still have at least two years to go out and act childish. Maturity can wait. Where did I put those ponies?

Chapter Two

To Class We Go!

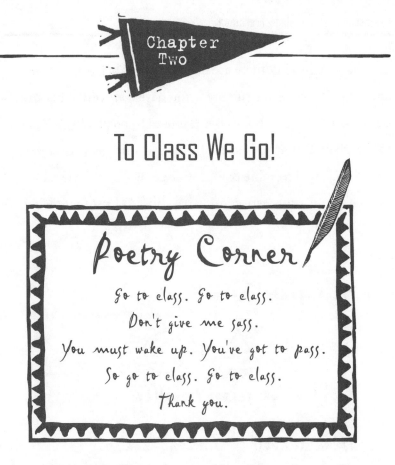

Poetry Corner

Go to class. Go to class.
Don't give me sass.
You must wake up. You've got to pass.
So go to class. Go to class.
Thank you.

Feel free to photocopy the above poem and
give it to everyone in your dorm, so they realize
just how serious this whole college thing is.

One of the major things separating high school from college
is that when you are in college you are no longer "going to
school." Now, you "have class." Don't get the two confused.
This is not the jump you made from junior high to high
school. High school was just a bigger and better junior high.
What we have here is an entirely different breed.

Yes, that's right kids, there are big differences between classes and school. School is structured. You have a schedule that makes sense—so does everybody else. You used to meet all your friends for lunch and sit at your special table every day as you talked about how Abercrombie & Fitch was going out of style and orange velour suits were coming back in. (At least that's what WE talked about.)

High school to college: a comparison

$$\triangle \neq \bigcirc$$

high school   college

High school to junior high: a comparison

$$\circ < \bigcirc$$

junior high   high school

Not so at college. Let's say you have a friend. Even if you don't, let's say for the sake of argument that you do. Now let's go a step further and say that you and your friend are going to the same college. Your friend plans to major in Marmot Psychology. You're getting a degree in Ice Cream

Manufacturing. Chances are, unless you get your friend's number and address the first day you're there and make firm and regular plans to contact him, you will never see him again.

Whereas, back in high school, your biggest classes would have 25 or 30 people, here you can expect freshman-level classes approaching 100 people. If you're at a larger state college, you can have classes in lecture halls holding thousands of students. The point is you can very easily feel like you have become a mere number in the vast university computer. The days of every teacher knowing you by name and giving you personal help every day are gone.

My first day of classes was an unusual experience. My first class started at 10:00 in the morning. Those of you in high school reading this book are thinking: *Ten? Thank the Lord! Maybe the world isn't really as bad as everyone has made it out to be.* But you'll be surprised at how early 10:00 is when you're in college. This is due largely to the fact that the official college day extends well into the wee hours of the following morning.

The night before, I set my alarm for 9:00 A.M. and went to sleep, my feet resting gently on the cover of my CD case. I drifted off to the rhythmic thumping of *Master P! Ghetto D!* being played loudly by our neighbors across the hall. That night I had unsettling dreams of professors giving me the evil eye, pushing buttons that made a trapdoor underneath my desk open, and being engulfed by the flames of hell as I fell into an eternal abyss. I woke up at 9:50, in a cold sweat. Then, seeing what time it was, I broke out into a rather warm sweat.

There is a fine art to getting dressed, cleaned, and arriving somewhere in ten minutes. Especially when the place you have to get to is five minutes away. It's like a dance. Guys: the key is the hat. Baseball, or any other kind of hat, will draw attention away from the fact that your hair could, if exposed, frighten small children. Girls: I have no idea how you deal with all that hair anyway. In fact, I don't really get how you do much of ANYTHING apparel-wise. So, I can't help you. But if you're late for class, and you don't mind looking like a guy, by all means read on.

Next: you must choose something without buttons. Buttons take at least an extra forty-five seconds. You are desperately going to need those seconds in about nine minutes. Just throw open the T-shirt drawer and pull something over your head. Do the exact same thing with the pants. Only don't pull them over your head.

Sandals are also important. These you can actually put on as you're running somewhere as fast as you can go. This may look awkward, but it is the most efficient way to get your feet shod. (I knew I could use that word in here somewhere.)

So, having gotten myself dressed and to class in the amount of time it usually takes to stop pushing the snooze button, I entered the building where my first college class was to take place. The building was impressive. Waco Hall, it was called. It had massive pillars, elegant windows, and impressive thingies that would make any architect jump for joy. I sprinted up to the door, bag in hand, ready to face the world.

Then I noticed the large throng of people milling about outside. I thought to myself: "Oh, maybe I'm not late after all!" Pushing through the multitude, I found my way to the door. There was a neatly printed sign saying, "Class canceled, come back Monday." I had gotten ready in world record time for a sign. Such is the college life. We sprint down the street putting on sandals, only to be told to come back Monday.

I think that's when it really hit me that I wasn't in high school anymore. Our high school was notorious for never canceling class. Our principal must have been in the postal service at one time: "Neither rain, nor sun, nor snow . . ." or however the phrase goes. If there had been an earthquake creating a great fissure surrounding the school and making it impossible to get there, everyone would have been given an unexcused absence for missing class. Then when someone complained to the teachers, they'd say something like, "Well, did you even TRY to cross the fissure?"

But here, without shame, a class was canceled for no other reason than being canceled. I was in shock. I didn't know what to do. I went back to my dorm room and stared at the ceiling for an hour. I finally shook myself out of the daze to go to my next class. It was a theater class. *At least that should be something comforting,* I thought.

So, feeling better about going to something familiar, I packed my backpack once again and set off into the campus frontier. I found my place in the theater classroom, and took out my pen and paper, all nice and ready to be a studious student.

Ten minutes later, there was still no professor. Twenty minutes later, someone who was not our professor came into the classroom, said the class we were in was now changing to another class, and that class was canceled today. I have never felt like such a lost puppy in all my life.

About half an hour after I left the building, I realized that classes being canceled for the day was in fact a good thing. I went down to the store, had an ice cream and reflected on my good fortune. I was oblivious to the storm brewing on the horizon.

The storm on the horizon was my 8:00 class on Tuesdays and Thursdays. Now, you people who are used to "school" starting at 7:30 will say, "Hooray! Another half hour to sleep in!" No, no, no. In college, if you go to sleep before midnight, you probably have narcolepsy. If your roommates go to sleep before 4:00 in the morning, well then I'd like to talk to you about trading roommates. "Sleep" is usually done between the hours of 4:00 and 7:00 in the morning. Now, perhaps you're saying to yourself, "Hey, that's all right, I'll just catch up sleep on the weekends." Once again, you are gravely mistaken. The weekends are not a time for sleep. Sleep on the weekends generally occurs during the hours of 6:00 to 11:00 A.M.

Please don't get me wrong—I'm not a "party guy." This lack of sleep does NOT have anything to do with partying. This is just a normal part of university life. The normal social activities, once reserved for the afternoon and early evening, now take place in the wee hours of the morning. Anyway, all this goes to say that an 8:00 A.M. class is a lot earlier than you think it is. If you think this doesn't really give you a lot of time to STUDY, try writing a book!

The very next day, my alarm went off at 7:15. I actually woke up this time. I seriously wished that I hadn't. I could have sworn I saw flames licking at the edge of my bed and Satan laughing in the background. Forcing my bloodshot eyes open,

I surveyed the room. There was bright sunshine streaming into the room. I hated it. The morning air smelled fresh and clean, and bluebirds were chirping outside my window. It was a good thing for the bluebirds that I didn't have an assault rifle handy.

I decided to clean myself up, and rolled out of bed, forgetting that I had chosen the top bunk. You would think that a six-foot drop would wake me up. I'm afraid not. After I remembered who I was, I got up and went to the mirror. About five minutes of staring at myself, I decided that shaving just wasn't that important to me today. So, I got dressed. I forced some food down my gullet and trudged off to class.

If there's anything I can't stand when I'm exhausted, it's happy people. Our psychology professor greeted us at the door with a cheery smile that made me want to bite his hand off as he handed me my syllabus.

For those of you who consider yourselves morning people, I apologize. You probably have no idea what I'm talking about— and are very confused as to why I'd be so evil in the morning. I'll try to relate it to something you can connect with: Imagine someone coming into your room, waking you up at 3:00 in the morning and working you over with a two-by-four. This would produce just about the same emotional reaction in you that waking up at 7:00 in the morning causes me. This is why I think many people say it's a good time to have your Bible study early in the morning. It opens you up for soul-searching questions such as "Why, God? Why?!"

Thanks in part to my 8:00 A.M. classes, I have developed different strategies to help me stay awake. I have developed what I call "the game method." This is really useful when you're extremely tired—if you don't mind looking a little silly. The game is very simple: Imagine that if you close your eyes, you will die. This can cause some strange faces, and don't be surprised if people ask you if you are having a seizure—I get that all the time.

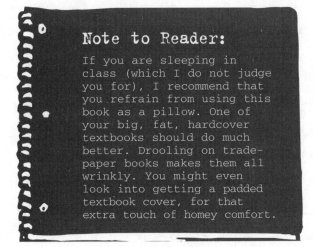

Note to Reader:

If you are sleeping in class (which I do not judge you for), I recommend that you refrain from using this book as a pillow. One of your big, fat, hardcover textbooks should do much better. Drooling on trade-paper books makes them all wrinkly. You might even look into getting a padded textbook cover, for that extra touch of homey comfort.

In the weeks preceding your freshman year, I'm sure you will hear this advice many times: "You need to attend class faithfully." Believe me, I know how tempting it is not to. Let me give you some friendly advice: Go. And remember that neither RiverOak Publishing nor I am responsible for the consequences of you NOT going to class. Thank you.

GOING TO CLASS!

College registrars have a ball creating students' schedules—because they are terribly fond of watching students (particularly freshmen) dash frantically from one side of campus to the other. For example, let's say:

(A) That your dorm is in the figure on the next page.

(B) The registrars are inevitably going to put your first class on the other side of the world.

(C) Then, your next class will be within sight of your dorm room.

Of course, the class after that will be in the vicinity of (D).

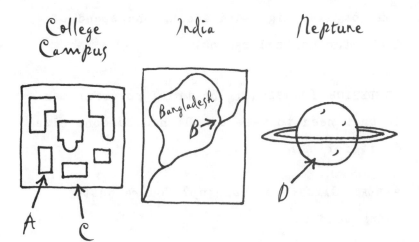

College Campus

India

Neptune

A C

Bangladesh
B→

D

WORLD SUMMIT ON WAKING UP FOR AN 8:00 A.M. CLASS

Here is what some famous people would have said about waking up for an 8:00 A.M. class, if they had thought about it:

ALBERT EINSTEIN: The amount of energy expended in waking up in the morning can be determined by multiplying the mass of the classes you had yesterday by the number of classes you have today, divided by the number of hours of sleep you got last night—and adding the speed of light for no good reason.

FREDERICH NIETZSCHE: The truly powerful man doesn't need to wake up. He has someone else do it for him.

ALBERT CAMUS: Why wake up? You're just going to die.

BILL CLINTON: What do you mean by "wake up?"

CONFUCIUS: Do not wake if you mean merely to go back to sleep. On the other hand, do not go to sleep if you will not wake up. Is anyone writing this down?

BUDDHA: How can you ever know that you are really getting up and not just dreaming that you're getting up?

DENNIS RODMAN: *#*%%#$!

SALVADOR DALI: Please help me. My eyes have turned to spiders, and I am melting.

Chapter Three

I Am Home, Yet I Am Not Home

Take it, it's good for you.

At this point in the narrative, I think I should make it clear to you that I am writing these chapters in chronological order. As of tomorrow, I will have been at Baylor five weeks. In some ways, it seems I've been here much longer. In others, I can't believe I've already been here that long. I feel I've come here and absolutely hit the ground running. For example, the day I arrived I had to go to a costume shop for a fitting, and rehearsals for the first university play started two days later.

I don't think I've taken a breath since then. For the past two weeks, I haven't come home from rehearsal earlier than 10:00 P.M., and I can essentially forget about the weekends. It feels like I'm in shock mode. I haven't really been able to think an individual thought since I got here. I have been incorporated.

My plan was to write a chapter a week for this book. This is week 5 and chapter 3.

All of the little neurons in my head that had it all figured out for high school are now an obliterated mess. I can actually feel them trying to cope. They're all running around in there, trying to come up with some way to hold all this information that has been shoved down my gullet. There's some little four-star general neuron in there going, "All right, boys! What are you, warthog neurons?! Hop to it! Adapt! ADAPT!"

I imagine that in a matter of time I will adapt, and all will be well. But right now I feel like I have applesauce between my ears. I'll tell you a very strange thing: I LIKE IT! AHHH HAHAHA! I'm under stress that would make a lab rat explode, but I'm loving it! It feels like I'm finally participating in LIFE—not just the filtered life that you get while living under the protection of your parents. This is the kind of life where, if you crash and burn, Mommy's not there to pick up the pieces. At long last I have taken the helm. It's exhilarating. I am under no restrictions. If I want to go out and play my guitar at 2:00 in the morning, in the middle of the freeway, *no one is going to stop me*.

Of course, this kind of freedom naturally produces idiots, such as those who play *MASTER P! GHETTO D!* AS LOUD AS THEY CAN AT

3:00 A.M! Sorry, I still get a little worked up about that. I'm thinking about going out and buying some Tom Jones or Slim Whitman, and seeing how happy my neighbors are waking up to that.

But therein lies the challenge: How to lead your life without losing control. Life gives you plenty of opportunities to go completely crazy without doing things that will mess it up. A random example: The other day I took my mattress to class with me. Why? Because I felt like it. It's more comfortable than a chair. (Of course, this was my theater voice class, so we were going to be spending the entire time on the floor anyway.) Most importantly, it's fun without being destructive. Sure it's crazy. Sure I get called "mattress boy." That's definitely a better story to tell the kids than, "Yeah, I was so drunk I fell out of a three-story window and didn't notice."

It's strange to me how in the short (and long) five weeks that I've been here, Baylor has become, in a very real sense, my home. It caught me off guard when I was going back to my dorm room and told someone that I was going *home*. Home for the past eight years has been a brick house surrounded by oak trees. Now suddenly I am referring to a small room shared with two other guys as home.

More importantly, my home is no longer shared with my parents. I think I always viewed my parents as Jedi knights.

They are honorable—the guardians of peace and justice in the galaxy. However, they do carry big light sabers. Now I am out of reach of those light sabers, and I must be accountable to myself. There is no higher moral power watching over me, except God. In a lot of ways, that's scary. God doesn't ground you. He just lets you do your own thing until you destroy yourself. That, ultimately, is a lot worse than getting grounded.

The important thing is this: College is now home. However, you shouldn't discard everything you had back home. One thing I have discovered to be an invaluable tool in keeping touch with the folks back home is the miracle of e-mail. It's easy, it's free (with your purchase of an Internet program), and it's a great way to stay in touch without running up the phone bill. In the five weeks that I've been here, I've probably sent thirty e-mails to my parents. Usually these messages say something enigmatic, such as "Sorry, I don't have time to type right now," but, hey, it's enough to keep Mom happy. I can also find out exactly how fast I'm draining my bank account, which is always a good thing.

Speaking of my bank account, I've spent plenty o' pennies calling my friends back home. A few of them are in Huntsville, one in Oklahoma, another in Arkansas. I'm really looking forward to getting back with them when Thanksgiving rolls around, but until then the priority is finding friends here.

This brings up the subject of "going home." The first weekend here, about 80 percent of the people I knew went home. Most of them had perfectly legitimate reasons for doing this, as they had forgotten important items, or they were being abused by their roommates. Then there were those who just missed mommy and daddy so much that they had to go back.

Don't get me wrong. There is nothing bad about missing your parents. It's natural, even healthy. It is not good, though, to mentally be back at home to the point where you aren't plugged in at the university. Our drama director said when his parents dropped him off the first day for college they gave him some of the best advice he's ever received. They told him not to come back until Thanksgiving.

This may seem a little harsh, but believe me, it makes the transition period between being your parents' person and your own person a lot easier. Once again, however, please don't confuse my advice for that of someone who knows what he's doing. This is what I see working for me. You might find it to be the best thing in the world to go home every weekend, but I doubt it. The relationships you form here at college will suffer if you don't give them some weekend time. You cannot live at home any longer. (Note: If you go to a college that is within sight of your house, this does not apply to you.)

I think the main lesson you're supposed to learn at college is how to be accountable to yourself and to God. You still have a home back home. There will never be a time in your life when your parents will be more supportive of you than this. Unless of course, you want to count changing your diapers and all the other stuff they did in your very early days.

The point is, with parents actively supporting you at home, it provides a good solid foundation for you to go out and explore the world. You know that if you make a mess, you still have to clean it up. But if you really need them, your parents will be there for you. It's a very comforting feeling to come home to my little room full of sweaty guys, knowing that there's still a place secured for me back at the little brick house surrounded by oak trees.

To reiterate: You are, effectively, starting over. If you're anything like me, you've been placed in a totally strange place with no one you know, and it can be rather frightening. Unless you want it to remain that way, you must get out there and start making friends, actively! I'm lucky because I was cast in the first play of the semester, and I automatically have a large base of people I'm spending great amounts of time with. I haven't found a best friend or a wife or anything, but I do kind of have a support group upon which I can build.

Let me sum things up at this point: College is a challenge.
I came from a place where I knew who my friends were—and
had a relatively good idea what I was going to be doing Friday
nights. Here it's like a mystery. Do I have any friends this week?
Or will I be in my dorm room eating cookies and feeling the
"Freshman 15" starting to take effect? (For those of you who
do not know, the Freshman 15 is the fabled and much-dreaded
15 pounds of weight gained in the average student's first
year of college.)

I suggest that you follow Billy Shakespeare's advice: "To thine
own self be true." Yes, you're out of the house, and you have
more freedom than ever before (unless you're stuck in
technical rehearsals). Remember who you are and what you
want to achieve. Go out there and participate in LIFE! Just
don't lose control and let yourself get sidetracked, doing things
you don't really want to do—simply because you can do them.

I think I'm going to stop preaching now. I've only been away
from home for five weeks and already I'm starting to sound
like a parent. I'm going to go do something foolish.
Goodbye for now.

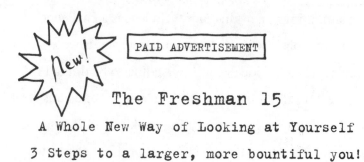

Studies and Social Life:
Are They Compatible?

I've heard all sorts of advice given about college, from everybody who's been there and a few who haven't. I'd say about 90 percent of it contains the word "study." Millions of courageous young men and women return home from college saying, "Yeah, oh my gosh, it's so much fun, but you have to read SO much." (If it is a girl saying this, add the word "like" before the words "Yeah, oh, so, you, and SO.")

Regardless of who tells it, the fact remains the same. You do, in fact, have to read more than you did in high school. Not only are you assigned more reading, you actually have to be responsible for remembering the material. I had friends in high school who thought profound reading was found on the backs of cereal boxes. They didn't even bother to go out and buy Cliff Notes. If this was you in high school, shame on you. Now go out and read *The Once and Future King* and *The Return of the Native* before I slap you. Those are good books.

There. I've had my little rant, and now we're moving on. The point is this: Studying must be done. If you do not study, you will fail. Right now this is becoming very apparent to me in my religion class. For every class we are expected to read a very large section of the Bible, sometimes even an entire epistle, and write a paper on it. Needless to say, with plays going on from 6:00 to 11:00 every night, finding time to do this without totally losing my mind and ignoring my other subjects is proving difficult. Don't get me wrong, I'm not complaining. I'm just asking you to write your congressman and tell him to sign a bill forcing all religion professors named Jeffery Hensley working at Baylor University to lighten up. (Note: These bills usually go through the bureaucratic process much more quickly if you include a hefty donation to a campaign fund.)

Before I came to college, I wasn't really sure what "studying" meant. In high school, people said they "studied" for tests and things. I suppose I may have looked over the material a couple of times, but I never had one of those intense nights slaving over books, which I'd heard so much about. This is the reason: In high school, if you listen in class, the teacher will generally go over anything you need to know for the test. It's a simple process. You read a chapter in a book; you come in and discuss it the next day. When you've discussed all the chapters, you will have a test on it. That's why people can pass the class without ever reading the book. It's practically like story time; the teacher sits and dictates the narrative of the book to you—and then explains what it means.

But now that you have entered the wonderful world of higher education, you will be responsible for learning and being able to manipulate the material on your own. I came into class expecting all the material that I was supposed to know handed to me on a silver platter. Instead, there was a *quiz* on the material waiting for me. Poopie.

This raises a big problem. This means that doing academic things is now going to have to cut into the time previously reserved for doing fun things—formerly known as any time that I was not in class. This is a major problem because, you see, I *need* that time. It's like coffee. If I don't get that time, I can feel my brain start to liquefy and run down to the base of my spine. Despite this need, there is still the fact that if I do not devote any time to studying, I will shortly find myself back living with my parents. Once you have moved out, this is not a place you want to go back to. I mean it's great—with the free meals and all, and I greatly miss being home. Just not enough to want to go back and stay.

"So," you ask, "how in the Wonderful World of Disney™ do I manage to juggle everything so that I can get all my studying done and still find enough time to have fun and avoid turning into a blithering, mindless (yet educated) idiot?" That's a good question, and I'm glad you asked it. It's one I've found myself asking repeatedly since I got here. It ranks right up there with "What kind of twisted genius did it take to invent the bagpipes?"

The answer (to the first question) is simple. Well, I take that back. It's not so simple. There are actually several methods you can employ to get back some of that valuable playtime. The one I use most frequently has very distinct advantages and disadvantages. What it involves, basically, is using the time you once allowed for play and now use it for studies. Then you take your playtime and put it in the time that you once used for sleep.

Look at this at 2:00 in the morning. You'll think it's the funniest thing you've ever seen.

One of the main advantages of this method is when you get into the wee hours of the morning, everything is funny. I mean everything. A psychotic murderer could break a bottle on the table in front of you, lunge at you with the intention of killing you, and you'd think it was the funniest thing in the world. I remember one particular night at a lock-in. My best friends and I went outside about 2:00 in the morning and spent an hour and a half throwing water on our faces. I have never laughed so hard in my life. That's just not something you can do in broad daylight, outside of a mental institution.

I have come up with many theories for this phenomenon. I think it may have something to do with lack of oxygen to the brain. I intend to ask my psychology professor about it. When I do, I'll let you know if there's a scientific reason for it.

Of course, a major downside to this approach is the destructive thoughts you get every morning when your alarm goes off. This method also causes problems staying awake in class, but there are steps you can take to ensure that you stay awake. For tips on this, refer to chapter 2.

Why insomnia is common among college students.

Food

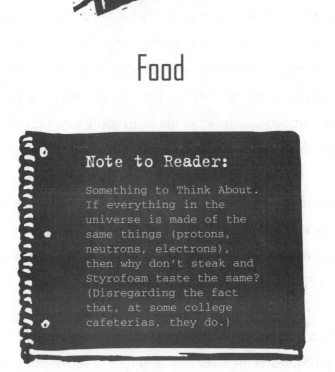

Note to Reader:

Something to Think About.
If everything in the
universe is made of the
same things (protons,
neutrons, electrons),
then why don't steak and
Styrofoam taste the same?
(Disregarding the fact
that, at some college
cafeterias, they do.)

One of the many deep, important, life-changing questions that
you will ask yourself when you get to college is one I find
myself posing on a daily basis: What do I eat today? Oh, if only
you knew how profound that question really is. I don't know
how it was where you came from, but at the house I lived in, a
typical meal was one that was prepared by my mother, and you
were expected to eat it, or starve. In the wonderful world of
"university fine dining," there are enough selections to make
even the most jaded young adult say, "Whoa."

Let me give you some background of the culinary arts in education. You will see that society has not come so far as one might think. I'm going to tell you a story. Back in medieval times, parents would send their children to school with something to nourish them, so they would better and more quickly understand how flat the earth really was. What they sent with them usually depended on what their trade was. The farmers would generally send their children off with some bread, beans, or other fruits of the field. Those who tended livestock would often provide a small portion of meat, such as the leg of a goat or a live rat in a bag. The blacksmiths would give their kids scrap metal, and so on.

This practice became commonly known as "taking a lunch," and it is probably still the safest and most surefire method of getting something edible at school. Now this method was good and lasted hundreds of years, and no one ever thought of doing anything else—until hard times fell on the land. The crops started to waste away; the cattle, goats, and rats became very lean and emaciated. The poor children's lunches started getting smaller and smaller, until the children at school became savagely hungry, and started fighting each other over peanut husks and rusty nails.

This continued until one day the king's son, Charles the Mediocre, was killed for his grain of rice. The king decided that enough was enough and something had to be done about the situation. He gathered up all of his greatest counselors, wise men, magicians, jesters, and playwrights and, with their help, came up with a solution. The next day it was decreed that lunch would be served at school to all who attended. In exchange, the firstborn son of every household would be enlisted to fight in the crusades.

This seemed like a reasonable agreement to the people, and the next day they sent all their children to school with hungry stomachs waiting to be filled. Behold! Lunchtime came around, and there was a great feast awaiting all the children. There was much rejoicing. All the children ate and were satisfied. However, in all the celebration, one thing was overlooked. The next day the chefs went back into their kitchens only to discover they had used up all the good food on the first day.

This posed a grave problem because they knew they had only a few precious hours until the children once again stormed into the dining halls awaiting food. They knew also that if the children did not receive the food that was promised them, none of them (and nothing of civilization) would survive the inevitable rage. So they set to work at a furious pace, making a broth and filling it with anything they could find—old shoes, broken glass, Black Death, live animals, dirt, lost children, paint, sewage, a pope, and even a few of their own number were thrown into the mix.

Just as the children started filing into the dining halls, the chefs covered it all with sugar and grease to give it the appearance and texture of food. They then served it to the hungry multitude, who ate it all so fast they didn't even notice the difference. The king, noticing the conservation in costs, commended the chefs and gave them all estates in Yorkshire, or something. Everyone lived happily ever after, except for those unlucky few who discovered what they'd actually been eating the whole time.

Now, the funny thing is that's really not so different from how a modern-day public high school cafeteria operates. At least that's how it was at my high school. If it was any different at your public high school, I suggest you: A) examine your sanity, or B) erect a shrine to whomever was in charge of your lunch program.

I've eaten some stuff that was scary. It wasn't just bad. It went past bad into evil. One day my entire tray moved 6 inches to the left without anyone touching it. How can you expect people NOT to think there are dark forces at work behind something that's called "chicken surprise?"

Lasagna Gone Wrong

A memorial for all the high school cooks
who lost their lives serving food
that sometimes bites back.

The reason I dredge up the horrors of high school cafeteria
food is this: The horrible days of sludge are over. College food
is actually (gasp) good! You can choose from a variety of
dandy morsels, ranging from the slices of lettuce that are so
popular among girls to the heaving mounds of saturated fat
so popular with me.

This does not mean that college food is flawless. You can
always find something to complain about if you're the kind of

person who likes complaining. Yes, there are some things to stay away from. They don't serve real eggs here; they serve what they call "egg-beaters." They're kind of a cardboard substitute for eggs. As for beating real eggs, they certainly don't. (By the way, take a step back and look at the word "egg." What a strange word. Whoever thought of coming up with a spelling like "egg?" Crazy.)

However, once you learn the ins and outs of your particular college food service, you can live quite passably off of what they serve. For example, this morning I had pancakes, biscuits and gravy, and a little glass of almost-orange juice. Then for lunch I had this really nice pasta thing with mushrooms and little green things, which was really good, and corn and other veggies. The wonderful thing is this: You don't have to get any one thing. If you go to the different cafeterias around campus, you are almost guaranteed to get just about anything you like. If you feel like pizza, there's plenty of that, and so on and so forth.

In the course of my choosing a college, we visited several institutions and made sure to test out their food courts. I say food courts because it really is like going to a mall, with its many little cubby-holed restaurants serving average-to-good tasting food. Well, that is exactly what college is—except you've never heard of any of the restaurants. And you don't have to pay for anything. (Well, technically you do, but you know what I mean. It's part of your room and board, so it doesn't seem that you're paying for it at the time.)

By the way, in the college food court I frequent most often, there are little venues by the names of Pan Geos, Rotisserie, American Grille, etc. If you go to one place long enough, you will develop meaningful relationships with the people who cook your food. It's always good to have a shoulder to cry on while you're waiting for your food. If you don't have enough drama in your life, try getting members of the cooking staff to date workers from other restaurants. This is always a good game, and it amuses me to no end. So far, I think we've established two and a half couples. Don't ask. It's a long story.

At first I was a little wary about devoting a whole chapter to food and eating. However, when you stop to think about it, this is not only a very important subject nutritionally, it is also an important social aspect of college life. Those of you who are going to rush for a fraternity or sorority, depending on whether you use the little boy's or girl's room, will find that it is very important where and with whom you eat.

There is a girl in my Costume Elements class. (Yes, I am learning how to sew. If you laugh at me, I will cry. I'm still a little touchy about this.) Anyway, there is a girl in my Costume Elements class who, shall we say, puts a very high priority on impressing those girls already in the sorority she wishes to pledge with. She is not "allowed" to sit with us at any time. I feel this is a little extreme, but it just goes to show you that eating at college carries more weight than you probably think it does.

If there's a college eating creed, I believe it to be this: Go out, have fun, eat anything you like, and try not to gain weight—unless that's what you want to do. Shoot, if your goal is to become as fat as nature will allow, then college is the place for you. More power to you. However, be careful you don't go off in the opposite direction. With no set meal times, it's very easy to miss meals—and possibly go for days without eating anything and not even realize it. After the first week I was here, I realized I had not eaten anything. This rather frightened me. So, I ate. That's the challenge I leave to you: Eat. Enjoy it. This is possible at college.

Dorm Life: A Boy's Story

> Biology experts say that the
> rain forest contains more life
> per cubic feet than any place on
> the globe. Obviously they have
> not been to "The DORM!"

I have decided that, due to *Life Magazine's* astounding recent
discovery that boys and girls are different, this chapter can
tell only half of the story. You see, life in a boy's dorm is so
incredibly different from life in a girl's dorm that writing a
chapter about "dorm life" in general would be as pointless as
throwing a hamster at a freight train (i.e. pretty pointless,
all extenuating circumstances aside).

To this effect, I have enlisted the help of a fellow Baylor
student who happens to live in a girl's dorm. This student is
living in the girl's dorm because she is, in fact, a girl. I have
solicited this person's help because, despite my persistent

efforts, the dorm officials at Baylor will not let me stay in the girls' dorm. (Those guys just will not listen to reason.)

All this is to say: If your driver's license says "Sex: F," then you can keep on reading the rest of this chapter for personal enlightenment, but don't be surprised if you don't understand what's going on. Warning: What you read will not be "cute." Scary things happen when you put a bunch of guys in a building together without their parents. OK guys, here we go. . . .

Behold the Dorm

So . . . you think you're ready for dorm life, do you? Mwahahaha. In psychology we are learning about what is called the "bystander effect." This basically states that people are not nearly as well equipped to deal with strange situations as they think they are. For example (and I can say this because it's just us guys reading, right?): You are watching a professional basketball game, and a guy pulls up for a shot that banks off the back of the rim, rockets out, and drills a bouncy cheerleader directly on top of her head, rendering her unconscious.

Now, it's very easy for you to stand up on your couch and proclaim you would never have taken that shot, and the fact this guy did obviously proves he shouldn't be in the NBA and you should. This is an error in judgment because if you or I or just about anyone I know were to set foot on the court with those guys, we would turn to applesauce within seconds. However, to the casual observer, the guy who took the shot appears to be a complete idiot. The point is this: There are some things in life that you think you might be ready for, when in fact, if you're anything like me, YOU ARE NOT. I have prepared a quiz that you may take to test your readiness to enter the chaotic world of living with a bunch of people you don't know.

The Dorm Quiz

(A) Have you grown accustomed to having just three and one-half square feet of space to call your own?

(B) Do you suspect that someone else is using your deodorant—and you don't care?

(C) Do you enjoy the sounds of muttering rabble outside your door at 3:00 in the morning?

(D) Do you get along with everyone all
the time, even when you're sick, tired,
and hungry?

(E) Are you the sort of person who enjoys
bathing in front of others?

(If you answered "yes" to any of the above
questions, please seek professional help.)

Here's the thing about living in a dorm. Take all your annoying
habits and character flaws, clone them a thousand times, and
that's what you'll notice running up and down the halls
directly outside your door. I have mentioned many times the
Master P enthusiast who lives across the hall from me. Don't
laugh just yet. There's going to be one on your hall, too. Maybe
two. Maybe you'll live with one. Maybe you are one, and your
roommate will bring along his treasured collection of Willie
Nelson CDs. The thing is—you're going to have to be able and
willing to compromise your personal living style to
accommodate others.

This was especially, monstrously difficult for me because I am
an only child. In my house there was always silence unless I
was making noise. When I reached the point where I started

becoming social (this did not occur until well into my teenage years), I started going over to friends' houses and realized how many *people* were running amok. There would be four, five, up to eight people in some instances. The sheer volume of people in these houses creates constant noise. The ones who were newer to the world would make high-pitched noises about malnourishment or whatever, which would cause the ones who had been in existence longer to make noises like "Shut UP!!"

A girl I dated in high school was the oldest of, like 700. Now, being a part of a family of 702 is bad enough, but to be the oldest . . . I shiver at the thought. For those of you who put up with that kind of thing, I salute you. Your tremendous efforts to maintain the little bit of sanity you have left go largely unnoticed. There should be a holiday in your honor. "Siblings' Day" it should be called. It's a day where you get to do whatever you want to whomever you want, and no one gets to tell on you. Just a thought.

So, needless to say, coming from a house where three was, in fact, a crowd, it's a little bit of a culture shock being placed in close quarters with hundreds of real-life functioning people. (I say that because there were other people who lived at our house through the years, but my parents never saw them, because they lived inside my head.) Until about two months ago, I had never brushed my teeth in front of anyone. If you've never done that before, you feel kind of weird doing it for the first time.

I think I truly realized that I wasn't in Kansas anymore one fine Monday morning. Now, here's a little something about Monday mornings. I hate them. Notice that I'm using the word "hate" here about Monday mornings. If they were gone, I certainly wouldn't miss them, except that without them, I would lose roughly fifty-two days of my life every year. So this story already has one mark against it just for happening on a Monday morning.

Anyway, I was on the way back to my room from the shower. I say I was on the way back because our showers are not located in or anywhere near our rooms. They are what we fondly refer to as "community showers." I'm not even going to talk about that. What I will say, though, is that if there is one thing about the morning that is acceptable, it is the shower. It is my personal happy time, during which I get to just stand under the water and soak in all the warmth, wake up, and listen to people threaten to kill me if I don't get out immediately.

This particular Monday morning, I had just gotten that day's batch of "happiness from the tap," and was headed back to my room to get dressed and otherwise prepare myself for the week's debut. Once there however, I discovered that both of my roommates had left, and, being the conscientious people they were, decided to lock the door. The thing about going to the shower is that, in order to get yourself properly cleansed, you need to rid yourself of all your clothing. While this state is good for cleansing, it is not generally accepted in social situations.

Although they did not know this, my roommates, by locking the door, had denied me access to my clothes. Having nothing but my towel, and with my tendency to think less than thirty seconds ahead, I hadn't brought my key along. My first reaction was despair. I thought about sitting down outside my door and crying until someone came along and offered help. Then it occurred to me that this is not something half-naked men do. I started asking myself, *What is it exactly that half-naked men do when they are in distress?* The answer? They panic.

So I ran into my R.A.'s (resident assistant) room in my disrobed state, unaware that they were having some kind of important meeting. There was this moment of unspeakable horror between the time I opened the door and all the important heads in the room turned toward me, and the time that anyone spoke. In this horrible silence I felt all the contents of my upper body exchange places three times. I have never been so grateful for a towel.

Then my R.A. said in that calm and cool tone of voice that means "I've got it all together and you obviously do not," "Do you need something?" Although my vocal cords had stopped working, my lips somehow managed to form the word "key." He said "Just a moment," and left me standing in my rather awkward state in front of a bunch of people who looked at least marginally important. Of course, when I am in situations like this I feel the stupid need to make petty conversation, which almost always makes things worse. I said something really dumb like, "Hi, I was just going to . . . I'm really, thinking . . . I'm naked*."

Note to Reader:

In the morning, when you are awakened by the sound of a hair dryer, repeat these words until your homicidal impulses subside: "I must not kill my roommate. They would throw me out of college. I'd have to clean up, too. I must not kill my roommate."

The R.A. finally got a key, and I haven't come out of my room since. The moral of the story is this: Things like this do not happen in private homes. Well, they might, but if they do, you've probably done something to deserve it.

Living in a dorm is a unique experience. You get to meet people. Very . . . interesting . . . people. Given the choice, I'll probably opt for getting an apartment next year, but I certainly don't regret getting a dorm room this year. At least not yet.

(*Naked, in this case, means naked underneath a towel.)

Chapter
Seven

Girls Just Wanna Have Fun

By Kristen G. Green, Special Guest Contributor

"I signed you up to stay in the 'cool' girls' dorm, Kristen!" my mother said emphatically during dinner a month or so before school started.

Come again? Girls' dorm? As in ALL girls' dorm? *Oh boy,* I thought sarcastically, *Now I can stay up with my newfound gal pals baking cookies and squeezing lemonade for our boyfriends while planning our weddings.* Needless to say, I was less than ecstatic. This was horrible; the "visiting hours" hardly existed and were strictly enforced. Even my father couldn't come and visit me outside the designated times. I became very bitter that some ruling fascist decided it was indecent for males and females to converse in a dorm. To a melodramatic teenager such as myself, this seemed a fate worse than death.

Not very long after arriving at college, I changed my tune. The girls on my hall and I enjoyed spontaneous '80s movie film festivals, making hot chocolate to keep warm in our arctic rooms, and the luxury of being able to walk to the shower in a towel. I soon became grateful that the visiting hours were minimal. Where else but in an all-girls' dorm can one feel the freedom to sing (off-key) *Little Mermaid* songs in the shower or lie in the hallway, hot rollers in hair, wearing your pajamas, and talking on the phone? Your hall-mates and R.A. quickly become your surrogate family, always there with a shoulder to cry on or pictures of their new boyfriends for you to inspect.

Several weeks into the school year, I ran for student government. This was before I had established a base of good friends, so I turned to none other than my hall-mates for help with my campaigning. It was like an episode of *Saved by the Bell.* In my eighteen short years I have never seen a group of people more eager to help with something that was not beneficial to them. We all pitched in, and in the process, got to know each other well.

I can't stress how important this is: Get to know your hall-mates and your R.A. Countless times my hide has been saved simply because I was in the good graces of the dorm authority figures. Your R.A. will in all probability be a very easygoing, social person who just wants to make sure you don't burn the building down. She wouldn't want the job if she weren't friendly, but regardless of how friendly she is, her job is to enforce the rules.

After the first several days went by, I visited my R.A.'s room with a bag of double-stuffed Oreo cookies and some basic questions about dorm life. No one can resist those little black and white sugar sandwiches offered with a smile. People always like food, and when your mouth is full it takes the pressure off having to talk too much. Besides brushing up on your conversational skills, introducing yourself to the local dorm authority figures starts you off on a good foot, and an edible token of your esteem will make sure you are sealed in their memory. This may prove to be very beneficial to you should you lock yourself out of your room wearing nothing but a towel (Zach) or orchestrate the kind of crazy stunts that college kids are notorious for pulling (me).

This also works at the beginning of the year to break the ice with all of the other new kids on your block. Remember that these girls will determine whether you regularly get a good night's sleep or stay up listening to their French horn as it resonates through every crevice of the building. You would be surprised at the wide variety of noise-making hobbies that come out of the woodwork at 2:00 in the morning when you have a big mid-term the next day. If you have already made an effort to befriend all of the potential cloggers, band members, and people who house epileptic elephants in their rooms, you have a much better chance of inducing quiet hours than the hermit at the end of the hall does.

Living in a dorm is an experience everyone needs to have at least once during college, but you won't always want to circle up with your hall-mates and sing Kum-Ba-Ya. I'm sure by now you've heard a million horror stories from your parents and older friends about how their roommate was from another solar system, or how they had a serial killer living across the hall from them, and the screams kept them up whilst trying to study.

But while you would have a better chance of winning the lottery and being struck by lightning than having 100 percent sane dorm-mates, it's not very hard to survive dorm life with all of your limbs and your sanity intact. Just like your family, your dorm-mates will have uncontrollably obnoxious quirks that will annoy you to the point you will think you've never left home. Remember, when you do butt heads with one or more of the residents around you, I have found that the most universally accepted peace offering is nothing more than the versatile bag of Oreos.

More on dorm life: It is a shame when you see two people stuck together who should never have been forced to live side by side. Some people are just not compatible. The French horn player across the hall had an affinity for Marilyn Manson, black clothing, and the Internet. This didn't mesh well with her Abercrombie & Fitch roommate, who stuck to a strict philosophy of matching her cashmere sweaters to her nail polish. (Note: Those little personality profiles colleges make you fill out so they can match you with a roommate must go right in the trash as soon as they get them.)

Anyway, I am sorry to report that screaming and gnashing of teeth could be heard from the Manson/cashmere room nightly. I bet they didn't start out conversing over a bag of Oreos. Too fatty, I suppose. I have heard that Nabisco has come out with a fat-free Oreo. Maybe this twosome should have tried them.

All in all, the girls' dorm experience is one not to be missed. You always have a group of supporters to wake you up when you forget to set your alarm and tell you when you have a run in your hose right before the big date. They are your cheerleaders, your partners in crime, your impromptu choral group. They can be the best assortment of mismatched friends you could hope to have. Wow, I'm being so sentimental. I think I'm going to make a mess for my roommate to clean up.

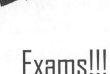

Exams!!!

(Or Tests, Depending on Your Vocabulary Preference)

Back in the days of Abraham Lincoln, schooling was very different than it is today. We have all heard the stories of the late president teaching himself to write by scrawling letters on a shovel with chalk. People were more honest back then. The students were gathered to *learn* the intricacies of a subject, instead of merely earning a grade on a sheet of paper.

The students would all be assembled, and the teacher would ask them, "Did everyone understand yesterday's lesson?" The students would respond, "Yes sir," or "No sir," depending on whether or not they understood the previous day's lesson. The children who said "yes" were given an A. The children who answered "no" were given failing grades, lashed forty times, and put in the stocks as an example.

This system worked perfectly until some wily child (probably an ancestor of mine) had the ingenious idea that if he said "yes" even when he didn't understand, the sessions of getting beaten to within an inch of his life would stop. He probably went on for years without being discovered, because in those days everyone adhered to ideals like honor, honesty, and hard work. Thankfully, today we have replaced these with laziness and entertainment.

After discovering that just saying you understood it, rather than actually understanding it, was a lot easier, this child spread his secret to all the other children. Their teacher was then amazed at how well the entire class was doing, and there was much rejoicing in the land. It was only when the entire town was full of people lacking the intelligence to name their own children that the educational community decided something needed to be done.

Their solution has been hailed by educators as the greatest invention since the No. 2 pencil. Students regard the solution as being definitive evidence that humanity has substantially digressed since the Garden of Eden. It is "the exam."

There are several differences in the kinds of tests you took in high school and the tests you take in college. Namely, the ones you took in high school aren't nearly as important as the ones you will take in college. In high school, you are tested about once every two weeks, or at the end of every chapter, or once every thirty seconds. This means that every test you take winds up accounting for about one-eighth of one point in your final grade.

In college, tests are rare and dreaded creatures with names like "mid-term" or "final" or "death." They occur three times a semester (if you're lucky), and each counts for roughly 85 percent of your final grade. Also taken into account, is the fact that you do not have any homework grades to speak of. You have a couple of quiz grades, but these are short little ten-question things that are combined at the end of the semester into a sum-total grade that is promptly thrown into the trash. Your quiz grades will not save you.

The trouble with tests is that I cannot tell you exactly how to prepare for them. I hate to use the word "study," because in many cases, there is no studying that can be done. In math, for example, either you know the material from paying attention in class or you don't. There is little hope for you to cram all the minutiae (thank you, Microsoft™ Thesaurus!) of calculus into your brain in a twenty-four hour period.

Books upon books have been written about taking tests, so I'm not going to tell you anything that hasn't been scientifically researched a thousand times over. Except this: Buttered toast and cats always land on the far side of the fence. I do know, however, there are two study techniques prevalent among college students, which I find to be equally useless:

1) **Panicking!** This will usually occur at that moment just about three minutes after you've gone to bed, turned the lights out, placed your body exactly in alignment, and have found the "perfectly comfortable position"—and never wish to move again as long as you live. Of course, at this very moment you realize you have the biggest test ever in the history of the human species in Molecular Biology Calculus Physics of Spam in the morning. Your brain takes a running leap about three and one-half feet out of your head, and you wind up drinking a lot of coffee, and trying to cram as much knowledge into that poor cranium of yours as you can. You come to class the next morning looking like some prototype human who has just evolved and crawled out of Lake Michigan. That is not the way to take a test.

2) **Apathy.** It is most commonplace for this to spring up about a week before the exam. If you are anything like me, you will be sitting at your desk, paying one-half to one-quarter attention, when your professor announces that you will be having a test over the last eighty-seven chapters of your reading material. A strange thing will happen. Maniacal

laughter will erupt from your throat, and you will feel elated because you know that you haven't read a single word for this class since you were handed your syllabus.

The maniacal laughter is because you know there is no way on earth that you're going to be able to shove all this information into your mind at the last minute, so you might as well give up. This will make it seem like a great burden has been lifted off your shoulders, and you want to go outside and frolic because you don't have to go and study. Please don't mistake this happiness as being normal. It is not joy; it is insanity. You won't be laughing when you get your test back and you can count your score on your fingers.

So, the best possible advice that I can give you is this: Pay attention in class. If you actually spend time thinking about what the professor gives you in the lecture or discussion of the material, you should do all right. If taking notes helps you, then by golly take them. I know right now all of you are nodding your heads, thinking, *Hey I've got it made!* Don't get me wrong, some of you probably do. Then there are those of us who have attention spans the size of a dead virus.

We of short attention spans always have the best of intentions. We sit down with our pens in hand and our notebooks open, all primed and ready to hang on every word that falls out of the mouth of our professor. Then, without realizing what's going on, we're suddenly in the Alesian Fields fighting off Vikings with a light saber. At least that's where I always end up.

There are some mornings that it's going to be a battle to keep your focus. Some mornings sleep and distraction are going to win. You must make sure to keep up.

Tests tend to come in waves. Actually, I think it would be a more accurate statement to say that they hunt in packs. My first wave hit about two weeks ago. First in psychology and then in Survey of the Bible. I was just sitting there, minding my own business, saving all the unwitting students sitting next to me from the hoards of attacking Vikings, when the professor decided to spring a test on us. Of course, if you want to get technical about it, he really wasn't springing it on us as the test had been in the syllabus since the beginning of the course. That's only if you want to get technical about it. The reality is, he sprung it on us.

The sole advantage to getting a test sprung on you a week in advance, as opposed to, say, thirty seconds before it's handed to you, is that the professors will sometimes be gracious to you. They may give you review sheets highlighting specific material that's going to be on the test. This is really helpful because then, instead of having to go back and read all 697 pages of the material that was assigned, you only have to be responsible for the 684 pages that are going to be pertinent to the test.

If your professor is feeling really generous, he or she might give you a review session. I have to question the helpfulness of these sessions because they tend to be somewhat vague. They usually go something like this:

You: "Hey, Mr. Professor (or Mr. Graduate Assistant), are we going to need to know how the theories of Freud and his contemporaries affected the field of evolutionary psychology?"

Professor: "If you know your reading and your notes, then you should do well on the exam."

You: "Yes, I know my reading and my notes, but are we going to need to know anything about Freud?"

Professor: "In order to do well on the test, you should go back and study your reading and your notes."

You: "Look here! Nothing you say is going to be used against you in a court of law! What good is a review session if you're not going to review anything?!"

Professor: "In the past, those who have done well on the test have been those students who have studied their reading and their notes."

So, it's safe to say that if you study your reading and your notes, and pay attention in class, you should do well on your test. There may be times during the class lecture when your professor says something like "Gee, this would make a good test question." Expect to see that material on the test in six or seven different forms. Here is a sample test question to give you an idea of what you're up against: Based on your reading about the human nervous system, what is the meaning of life?

In conclusion, I'd like to say that I like pizza. If you have any further questions or comments about taking tests, please feel free to call my father, Jack Arrington, at 1-800-AUTHORITY. He'll make sure you study. Trust me.

Alternatives to Studying
for a Test

(A) Failing

(B) Dropping out of college

(C) Alien abduction

(D) The Apocalypse

(E) Hospitalization

(F) Winning the lottery

(G) Death

Organization and Responsibility

Good morning. You are eighteen. You are on your own. The older people you used to live with and told you what to do all the time are no longer around. When your alarm clock rings, no one is going to make you get up and do anything. When there is homework to be done, no one is going to make you do it. If you are in the mall with all your money and a giant autographed poster of the Backstreet Clones catches your eye, no one is going to stop you from buying it. (But for the sake of everything that's Christmas, I hope your conscience does.)

This is the reality that has come upon you. Unless you take action, your room will never be clean, your bed will never be made, and your clothes will never be washed. Those of you (myself included), who would rather get amoebic dysentery than do housework, will realize there are problems when three weeks into the semester, all you have to wear is a sock and you cannot find your floor.

The solution to this problem is one that my parents have been trying to pound into my skull since about six minutes after I was born. Organization and responsibility. I am almost ashamed that I, the "king of leaving things in random places," am writing a chapter on organization. Not to mention responsibility. Responsibility is one of those "grown-up" words that your parents say to you when you're six after you've broken Mr. Schmelding's window with a baseball. I am almost shocked to hear myself say it, much less type it in a book and refer to it as a good thing.

However, it must be a necessary component of your life if you're going to survive at Ye Olde Université. I don't really feel qualified to give you tips on how to organize your life, because mine is just about as organized as a nuclear test site. Plenty of books on organization have been written, and I don't think I could add anything new to the discussion, so if you want an extensive list of things you can do to help yourself, please seek out your local bookstore or Tony Robbins or once again, my father. What I can do, however, is give you examples of how disorganization can cause you great distress, mental anguish, and in the end, drive you more insane than the people who wrote the tax code.

For example (and this does relate in the end): One item in the unending list of ways that college is different from high school is that you have to register for classes every semester. Even the "year-long" courses are treated as if they are two different classes. This means that many classes last only one semester. When these classes run out, you must decide what classes you're going to take next, get advised for them, and register for them. In order to get in the school computer, you have to do this about a month before the end of the semester (at Baylor, that's November 10). According to my Microsoft® Windows 95™ taskbar clock it is now November 16, 1999.

Coincidentally, this is the same clock that in about a month and a half, will reset to 1900, causing my computer to reach critical mass and explode. Of course, by the time you buy this book, "Y2K!!!" will have already come and gone, so either civilization is fine and moving along the way it always has been, or you're setting the paper from this book on fire and using it to cook some wildebeest that you caught with your bare hands and a spear. (Author's note, June 14, 2000: *Y2K? Ah hahahaha.*)

As you can see, I am easily distracted. The title for this book should be *Zach's Guide to . . . Hey! Something Over There Looks Cool! Let's Go Do That!* This is probably a major contributing factor to the fact that it is six days after my registration date, and I have not taken any steps to registrate myself.

Anyway, as I was saying before I so rudely interrupted myself, I am several days late for registrating. (At this point, my Microsoft® Spellcheck™ is informing me that I am making up words all over the place here. "Registrate" apparently is not a real word. Who knew? The Microsoft® Spellcheck™ Suggestion© Thingy®™© says, "Registrate: No suggestions. Except one: Stop inventing words that don't exist, get yourself a dictionary, and grow up.")

Narrator: *And now, chastened by his old arch nemesis, the Spellchecker, our hero girds his loins and steels himself to write the rest of the chapter. With fire behind his eyes, and the ever-present college fatigue settling in his brain, he presses on.*

Okay, then. There are several major problems with registering late. The first problem is there are several million other people who are just as disorganized as you, and they're all rushing to get their classes before you do. This means the space just in front of the registrar's office is going to look like a scene from feudal Japan. People who not four hours ago were your dearest friends now turn on you with ferocity. Eventually, however, you delude yourself into thinking that you see the light at the end of the tunnel when you have almost reached the registrar's desk.

The reason I say "deluding yourself" is that's exactly what you are doing. This is when the real frustration begins. You have all your classes nicely figured out, and your schedule is perfect and neat and tidy. Your nice and friendly schedule says that none of your classes will start before 10:00 A.M., and you have all the best professors in the school. The only problem with this: All the good students who pay attention to what's going on at school, and therefore registered on time, want the same classes.

Are you wondering why I said "you" in the preceding paragraph? I didn't mean you, the reader. The "you" is really "I." From this point on, I will not try to hide behind the camouflage of pronoun displacement. *I* didn't register on time. You, please don't make the same mistake.

So anyway, the point is that if *I* don't register on time, *I'll* get stuck in a bunch of courses that start at 5:30 A.M. and are taught by graduate students who just flew in from Mogadishu and talk in accents so thick they can't even understand themselves. Another downside: These classes are going to be filled with the kind of people who, just like me, didn't register until six days after the deadline.

This is just one of the many episodes I have had to endure on account of my irresponsibility. I have the unique ability to lay something down, and if I blink or sneeze, it's gone. The other week I was going to a Creed concert. I was very excited about this. I bought my tickets and everything. I wound up not going to the concert because somehow twenty minutes before the show I lost my tickets. If I were someone else, and I knew me, I would have been yelling and slapping me. Unfortunately yelling at yourself in public comes across as rather strange. So I went to a movie. The movie was okay.

I AM _____

Put your name on the line
above so you can remember
who you are when you
get confused

The other day I lost my car. It is rather embarrassing to lose something that weighs twenty times more than you do.

A number of you may say, "Oh, please, he's making this up. Who loses a car?!" This is because you don't know me. Those who do know me just laugh. If earth were populated with Zach Arringtons, we'd lose it. I mean literally, we'd lose the planet. One day we'd wake up and not be able to find it. It's really that bad.

Here's how I lost my car: I was in somewhat of a hurry because I was late for a rehearsal. I rushed out of my dorm to the space where I had parked my car. Lo and behold, it was not there. I knew for a fact that I had parked my car there. I even remembered the cars I had parked next to. One of them was approximately half an inch off the ground and had wheels smaller than my head, and the other had this neat little bumper sticker on it that said "Feed the Homeless to the Hungry." I thought that was cute, especially since I think it was on the bumper of a car that belonged to a member of the student government. These are the kinds of people who deserve to be in power.

I was in great distress. Not only did it not look like I was going to make it to rehearsal on time, it looked like I wasn't going to be going anywhere—ever. I could just hear the phone conversation. "Hi, Dad, this is your son. Yes, I'm fine. There's been a little bit of a mix-up. I seem to have lost the car."

Then comes the part when my parents come through the phone to kill me.

Fortunately, after spending a good thirty minutes freaking out, I remembered that I had driven it to the theater building, forgotten I had driven it there, and walked home. So I walked over to the theater, and there was my car, looking very smug. After kicking it in the bumper a few times for letting me be so reckless, I drove to my rehearsal. I apologized for my tardiness, explaining that I was severely mentally handicapped, and needed to be dragged out into the field and shot. Everyone thought this was a great idea, and the whole episode ended in laughter, just like on *Scooby-Doo.*

The reason (and there is one) that I tell you all this is I do not want you to become the nervous wreck that I make myself at times. Do whatever it is you think you can do to help yourself. Swallow your pride and break out the Post-it notes. Go see an advisor. Get an upperclassman to help you out with organizing things. If you're feeling especially daring, you can even try cleaning your room on your own once or twice. I have tried this, and it's actually somewhat rewarding until thirty seconds later, when it looks exactly like it did before you spent the six hours cleaning it.

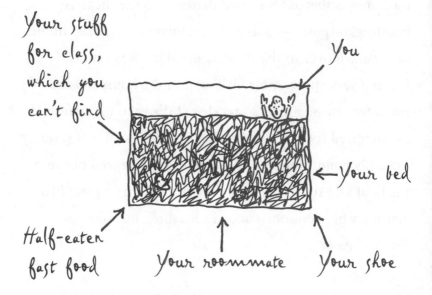

Cross-Section of a College Dorm Room
(This is the way it really is.)

Your stuff for class, which you can't find

You

←Your bed

Half-eaten fast food

Your roommate

Your shoe

College is a huge deal (and ordeal). There are an incredible number of loose ends that, instead of relying on your parents to tie up, as I did, you're going to have to start tying yourself. A key ingredient in keeping yourself sane—write things down. The moment you think, *Hey, that's easy, I'll remember that,* you lose it. Pretty soon you start forgetting what assignments you had, what classes you're taking, and what your mother's name is.

To sum up, organization and responsibility are your friends. Even though they're annoying, they are necessary. Now go to your room and think about what you've just learned. There, now that I totally sound like your parents I'm going to leave you with one final thought: What would happen if everyone in the world took a huge breath all at once?

Campus Christianity

As the author of a book that is being published under a
Christian label, and indeed being a practicing Christian
myself, I feel that it is important that I discuss Christianity
in *Confessions of a College Freshman*. Unfortunately, when
writing a book about real life, one cannot help but alight on
some touchy subjects. When one does, the best one can hope
for is not to step on too many people's toes. Without further
ado, here I go.

This chapter was inspired on a particular Wednesday night
when my friend Claire and I were sitting around shooting the
breeze. As is common when talking with Claire, the
conversation turned toward spiritual matters. This time it
turned toward some of the unique obstacles that face kids
raised in Christian homes, and then go out on their own to
fend for themselves.

You see, the perspectives of a life-long Christian and someone
who converts to Christianity later in life are totally different.

Those raised from birth in a Christian home, as myself, have never known anything but Christianity and can't imagine what life is like without it. For their entire lives they have been taught that Jesus is the Way, the Truth, and the Life, and there is no other truth besides that. What we don't really expect to find, but frequently do on today's college campuses, are people who have completely thought out their world views, have a logical system of how they believe the universe works—and Jesus is nowhere to be found in it.

Here's the problem: What happens when a bunch of fresh-faced Christian kids who have never really seriously tested what they believe come face to face with a bunch of highly intelligent non-Christians who have thought through every step of the process and want to "enlighten" these repressed Christian children? The result is that these Christian kids get overwhelmed. Either that or they get frustrated when they are ineffective at reaching their peers, who, although they're Taoists, know more about Christianity than the Christians do.

I'd like to propose what I call a new breed of Christian youth. I'd like to see a force of kids who can not only rip through a sword drill, but can also hold intelligent conversations about other religions—and know *why* they believe Jesus is the only Way.

You have no idea how much it pains me to hear some of the discussions in my religion class. I am convinced that in every religion class there is at least one kid who sits in the back and will argue against anything that seems like a point. We had one of those kids in my class, and it was scary to see how ill-prepared the rest of the class was to deal with that kind of a situation. The general opinion of that contingent was that "Jesus loves me this I know, for the Bible tells me so." Beyond that they had no real justification of their faith besides some vague notion of what they "feel" or how it had changed their lives.

If we're going to make any kind of impact on our college campuses, we need more substantial arguments than that. We have been raised to believe that the Bible is ultimate truth, and there's never any reason to question it. However, we must realize that there's a whole world of people out there who have been raised to think that the Bible is dead wrong, and anyone who believes in it is an intolerant, hate-filled bigot.

The first step in creating this new breed of young Christians is a dangerous one. In order to get on the same plane as the people you will be dealing with in spiritual matters, you need to begin with the premise that Christianity is wrong. Now before you start burning this book and call RiverOak Publishing, hear me out. You believe that Christianity is the truth, right? How do you know that it's the truth? If you've never tested it, you're just walking in blind faith. As much as blind faith is to be lauded, it's not going to get you anywhere in a serious philosophical conversation.

If you work through every argument that you can find against Christianity and still come out intact, how much stronger will your faith be? I'll be honest—I'm still trying to work my way through some issues about Christianity that are really tough to understand. "Slaves obey your masters." What's that all about? But if you can start from the standpoint of "Christianity is not true" and work your way through every alternative, coming to the conclusion that Christianity IS true, then how much stronger is your testimony for Christianity going to be? Let me tell you—a lot.

The best witnesses in the world come from people who at one time, lived a life that was a polar opposite from the Christian walk. My father is one of those people. Many times the reason these people's walks with Christ are stellar is that they were desperate and hungry for God and had to go out and FIND the truth. Maybe you're one of those people. As for me, I've had the truth served to me on a silver platter all my life, so I find it much harder to communicate clearly with people from other viewpoints.

What I began to realize when I left home is that the world is a big scary place. It's like this big game we are thrown into and told to start playing. We don't know the rules, we don't know how to play, and we don't know how to win. The fortunate few of us who were given the rulebook sit back and sometimes forget that there are people out there who are desperate for answers.

They don't necessarily want my answers. That's human pride. They'd rather find the answers for themselves. They'd also rather cling to familiar faulty answers than try to grasp new ones. Truth isn't dependent on faith, and let me tell you, we'd better be glad that it ain't. There are plenty of Muslims out there whose faith in Allah would put many Christians to shame. But, as they say, no matter how hard you believe it isn't raining, you're still going to get wet.

Let me assure you there is plenty of logical reasoning and support behind Christianity. Jesus was a reliably documented Jewish carpenter who lived and taught during the first century. The truth is still the truth. But faith and logic need not be mortal enemies. In fact, if any progress is to be made in winning others to Christ, we need to realize that they are inseparable. This is important on the college campus more than anywhere else. If you go to a secular college, there are going to be professors who are not only NON-Christians, they will be blatantly ANTI-Christian and will do everything they can to bend your malleable mind away from it.

One of the most prevalent ideas on college campuses today is that of ethical relativism. This is a really hard one to fight because it basically says "What's right for you is not necessarily right for me. You do your thing, and I'll do mine." With people who profess this, it doesn't matter how much you say, "The Bible tells you so." They'll just say, "That's great, and you can believe that all you want, but Confucius tells me this. . . ."

There will be really intelligent kids your age who have outrageous views, and you may have to defend your beliefs against these characters. If you don't have a ready defense against these various attacks and beliefs, you're going to feel very confused and possibly betrayed because you were never exposed to these ideas before.

Now please don't mistake this chapter as a call to forsake your morning devotions and stop praying before meals. Your heart is far and away the most important thing to God. However, a strong heart and a weak mind can get you pretty lost and confused, and your witnessing potential is going to be greatly reduced because of it. So, go out and question your beliefs.

(In a healthy way, of course. Just because you're doing a spiritual self-examination does not mean you should turn your back on God.) Make sure you know why you believe what you believe.

Once you have a system of beliefs with sound judgment behind them, you'll be unstoppable. Now go out there and change the world.

A Day in the Life

Ugh.

Note to Reader:

This chapter starts out
with an "ugh" because that
is exactly what is going
through the head of the
author right now. You see,
yesterday the author
decided it was a good day
to go play basketball at
the Student Life Center.
Also, apparently this huge
6'5" guy who probably
played for Baylor on a full
scholarship decided that it
was a good idea to
go play basketball at the
Student Life Center also.

Since the author, at 6'3",
is not exactly lacking in
height, the other members of
the author's team thought it
would be a great idea for
the author to guard this
"hulking mound of flesh."
The author wasn't too pumped
about this, but agreed
anyway. The game started,
and the huge hulking mound
of flesh proceeded to beat
the ever-loving life out
of the author.

(continued . . .)

Huge Hulking
Mound O' Flesh
4

(continued...)

Things finally came to a head
when, as the author was
trying to make a line drive
to the basket, the huge
hulking mound of flesh
decided that it wanted to
take the author's leg home
and hang it on the wall.
It jammed its huge hulking
mound of knee into the
author, which must have been
equipped with a spiked metal

(continued...)

(continued ...)

"flesh mauler" because it
flung the author against the
far wall, after which he had
the distinct feeling that his
leg had become the home of a
colony of bees. Being a guy,
our author-hero shook it off
and played the rest of that
game, which he won. However,
as soon as the author stepped
off the court it became very
obvious that he wasn't going
to be moving all that much
in the upcoming days. Right
now the author's leg is
adhered to his body by some
string, Ace bandages, and
ticky-tack. Such is the
meaning of "ugh."

Well, greetings once again, gentle reader. This chapter is
designed to give you a specialized tour of a day in the life
of a college student, namely me. The day that I am about
to describe is not one day in particular, but sort of a collage
of days, blended together to give you the finest taste
of what awaits you on a typical college day with only
three grams of fat.

The Day Begins

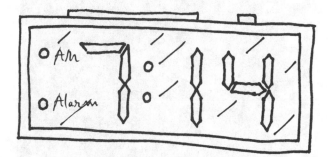

The face of evil.

7:15 A.M.: Alarm clock begins its sadistic awakening ritual. Sometimes (and this is an omen that I am going to have a really bad day), I'm fortunate enough to wake up just before the alarm goes off. One moment I'll be having this wonderful dream that I'm a cowboy chasing donuts across space, and the next moment, for no apparent reason, I am suddenly awake and staring at my clock, which says 7:14. The look that I get on my face at this point is very similar to the look that bomb technicians get in movies when the bomb is going to explode in three seconds, and they know they can't defuse it.

I get this look because, particularly at 7:14 in the morning, my alarm clock is every bit as annoying as a bomb. So I lie there, staring my clock down in complete hatred, trying to cling to my last fleeting moments of freedom. Then the clock gets this really smug look on its face and starts going, "beep. beep. beep. beep." I sit there staring at it, trying to will it to self-destruct, but it just keeps spitting beeps at me. There's really nothing that I can do about this because it takes about five or six minutes for my brain to warm up to the point that I can move my arms and legs.

7:20 A.M.: My arm finally realizes it is receiving messages from my brain telling it to move and does so with the speed of a dying three-toed sloth on morphine.

7:22 A.M.: Arm actually reaches alarm clock and turns it off. I stare at it stupidly while my brain is saying, "Good living fat Buddha, I'm awake." My left arm then decides it's time to take action, and rolls me out of bed—once again forgetting about the 6-foot drop.

7:25 A.M.: I regain consciousness, grab my towel, sandals, and little shower caddy and head to the restroom for some "happiness from the tap." One must always be wary of the shower floor. It's inhabited by strains of bacteria the size of household pets. If one of them gets on your feet, it's all over. The showers here are really zealous. Once you turn them on, they are determined to drill a hole directly through your body.

If you try to turn them down they punish you by covering you with water that would make Eskimos shiver, sometimes shooting chunks of ice at you. This is sometimes, however, just what you need to get your engine running.

7:35 A.M.: I finish completing my morning rituals and head to get breakfast. After eating my breakfast and leaving the cafeteria without opening my eyes, I brush my teeth and head to my first class. I generally regard this as a big mistake. In fact, looking back on my life, there isn't much that I have done before 12:30 P.M. that has been beneficial to me in the long run.

8:07 A.M.: I stagger into my first class of the day (psychology), totally unprepared for the daunting task awaiting me as soon as I cross the threshold—finding my seat. Actually, to tell the truth I find psychology really interesting. I was reading this section on schizophrenia, and it really struck me. Allow me to read you a quote from my textbook. This quote is from a young woman suffering from schizophrenia, which is described as the "cancer of the psychological world." This young woman says:

"This morning, when I was at Hillsdale Hospital, I was making a movie. I was surrounded by movie stars. The X-ray technician was Peter Lawford. The security guard was Don Knotts. The Indian doctor in building 40 was Lou Costello. I'm Mary Poppins. Is this room painted blue to get me upset? My grandmother died four weeks after my eighteenth birthday."

Now the reason this caught my attention was the fact that this sounds exactly like something that I'd say. I mean, I wouldn't be surprised if the textbook had placed my name by the quote. One night my friend handed me one of those little tape recorders with the mike, and said, "Just say something random." What is on that tape today is about twenty minutes of the weirdest monologue that has ever walked the face of the earth. (I'm convinced it's walking.) I don't know whatever happened to that tape. It probably weirded itself out of existence.

9:20 A.M.: I wake up and stagger out of that class and on to my next one, religion. This is a course most of you who are attending secular universities won't be required to take. It would be a pretty interesting course for me if everyone in the class were not a raving lunatic.

11:00 A.M.: By this time I am at least awake enough to state my first and last name in the correct order. Coincidentally, this is also the exact time my religion class lets out, so I am no longer required to think. I usually will go back to my room to check my e-mail, which is a vital component of my life, and then get something to eat.

11:30 A.M.: I get something to eat. As I have stated in earlier chapters, there are many choices for getting fed on campus. By this point in the semester, I have pretty much narrowed it down to two choices: "The same thing I get every day" or "something else." I don't think there has been a time in the last couple of weeks where I have gone with the "something else" option. A man needs stability.

1:00 P.M.: My acting class begins. This is a very interesting class that consists of thirty-six college students lying around on the floor and breathing. (The wonders of higher education!) It is only after this class is over that I am truly free.

1:50 P.M.: I am truly free, except for all the other stuff that I have to do, such as costume or running crew, rehearsal, writing a book, or, if my stars are lucky, study. Given all these choices of using my time wisely and being a productive little human being, I usually choose to sit around and play on my computer. I would go out and do stuff with my friends, but they always give me this line about, "They have to study." I personally think it's a cop-out but, oh well.

3:45 P.M.: I change clothes and drive over to the Student Life Center to play a little basketball, only to be greeted by the hulking mound of flesh who would like nothing better than to have my spleen as a lawn ornament.

5:00 P.M.: I drag myself back to my room and attempt to read my psychology text without bleeding on it. I read about a paragraph and a half before deciding that it's hopeless and that "I'm never going to really need this anyway," Then I play Tetris until my brain falls out.

6:25 P.M.: I realize that I was supposed to be somewhere at 6:00.

6:30 P.M.: I arrive at my costume crew. Let me explain costume crew to you. Basically I help with the scene changes by taking this guy's clothes on and off. It's really exciting stuff. There's another costume crew in which you actually sew the costumes, but they know better than to get me involved with that. When I'm sewing a garment, I generally regard it as a success if I don't sew my fingers together.

10:00 P.M.: I am done with my costume crew. (Yes, it takes that long.) I go home, wipe the blood off the psychology book and attempt to launch into it again. After about two sentences and a picture caption, I decide once again that it's time to give up.

10:01 P.M.: Tetris begins.

1:15 A.M.: I look at the clock and realize that it's 1:15 A.M. I also realize that this is kind of ironic because it was only eighteen hours ago that I promised myself I would never again go to bed after 8:30. Actually, I tried that for a period during the school year last year, and I'm telling you people that I discovered the "secret to eternal happiness." (Taking into consideration God's whole plan of salvation, etc.) The "secret to eternal happiness" is going to bed before 9:30 every night. I dare you. Try it. You'll wake up singing like a bluejay every morning. The only problem with this secret is that it's totally impossible to keep. It lasts a week. Maybe two, and then, inexplicably, you find yourself once again going to sleep half an hour after you get up.

1:47 A.M.: I finally get everything set and go to bed, visions of sugar-plum fairies and the whole nine yards dancing around in my head. I start gently dozing off and am at total peace until...

1:48 A.M.: All the other guys in the dorm decide that this is a great time to get out their bazookas, bulldozers, and herds of water buffalo and play with them in the hall. I have never actually gotten out of bed to verify that this is what is going on, but judging by the noise out there, that is the least scary thing I can imagine.

5:30 A.M.: I actually get to sleep.

7:14 A.M.: I wake up exactly one minute before my alarm goes off.

Note to Reader:

Regarding days like these—although I did get very good at Tetris, topping 160,000 points—this kind of day, and others like it, took a toll on my grades. My first-semester grade point average (GPA) was 2.5. My scholarship was in danger, since I was required to maintain a 3.0 GPA to keep it. Fortunately, I earned a 3.6 for the second semester, and my final average was 3.00000. This is a testament to many long hours of study and hard work. You really have to sacrifice to make college work.

Homecoming and School Spirit

(Ra, Ra, Ra, Be True to Your School)

I have noticed a funny thing this week. It is a phenomenon that is very obvious if you look at the Baylor parking lot during Homecoming or Parents' Weekend. There are an inordinate amount of green cars in the parking lot. The people coming out of them all seem to be wearing shades of green as well. This doesn't seem to be too odd until you take into consideration that Baylor's school color is green (and gold, but no one ever thinks of that). Now, the people wearing these clothes, specifically bought to show support for Baylor University, are not the people that actually attend the University. These are the parents of the people who go to Baylor; people who graduated thousands of years ago and still have this notion of school spirit.

I got the subtitle for this chapter from a Beach Boys' song. The lyrics go like this: "Ra, ra, ra, be true to your school." I have always thought this song was a little odd. In this day and age, one might as well just be singing a song that says, "Ra, Ra, Ra, pay your taxes early." It seems kids are getting increasingly tired of going to school. I'm not trying to say that I'm any different. During my glorious elementary years, the last thought that would waft through my childish brain before I delved into peaceful childish sleep would be of a squadron of B-12 bombers vaporizing the school during the night.

When one goes to high school, the school spirit picks up momentum a bit, albeit only a little, and only when it gets one out of class. The school marching band plays rousing themes, there are pep rallies for various basketball and football games in which everyone is excused from classes to yell for a while— and sometimes people actually know what their school colors are.

← Random balloon of happiness

If you think about it, school spirit exists for three reasons: sports, parents, and cheerleaders. Sports are the key ingredient here. Without them, you would quickly lose the interest of both the parents and the cheerleaders. As noble a pursuit as chess club is, it will unfortunately never be the kind of rallying event that a football game is. Although I don't know from personal experience, apparently there is nothing more gratifying in the world than to watch your child get the snot pounded out of him by someone else's child. This is a reality that seems common to all parents of football players. I do know from experience, however, that watching the cheerleaders encouraging the violence is, in itself, a wholly edifying experience.

All of these factors come together within a person's soul to form a bond with the place that makes all this activity possible—the school. This feeling tends to intensify during the college years. This is probably because when you are at college, your school affects every facet of your life. You live at your school. All the people you live with and interact with on a daily basis go to your school. It's literally like being a part of a small, self-contained city.

The reason all these thoughts of school spirit are drifting through my mind is that it is Homecoming season. School colors across the nation are flying high. Everyone is going through the little rituals of having parades, lighting bonfires, and basically encouraging general gaiety.

Every school has its own little way of celebrating Homecoming. It really depends on the school you attend. If you go to a place like Tomball Community College, you probably celebrate by sitting around and staring at your fellow students. If you go somewhere like the University of Texas, you celebrate with massive amounts of whooping, hollering, and formulating ways to wreak havoc on rival schools.

We at Baylor find that it suits us to memorialize this special occasion by honoring a number of strange traditions that are functions full of joy for those who love school spirit—and make the cynics scoff. It all starts when the freshmen are given the "eternal flame." The title of "eternal flame" is not entirely appropriate for the little candle, however—it tends to extinguish about six times a year. The reason it goes out is that an elite group of freshmen is charged with the task of making sure the candle *doesn't* go out. Things go very well for them until an elite group of upperclassmen decide to show the freshmen exactly what makes them so fresh.

The poor little raggedy band of freshmen sits around the poor little raggedy candle with its little fiery tongue of school spirit lapping just above their shoulders. They sit there for three days straight, twenty-four hours a day, waiting. It gets to be around 3:00 in the morning on the second day, and a senior appears in the foliage. The freshmen become tense. They stare at him, and he stares right back. That's when the attack comes. Not from the front, but from the sides *(wssshhh!)* come the other twelve seniors they didn't even know were there. Seniors are pack hunters, you see. They use coordinated attack patterns, and are out in force today.

The seniors generally use a liquid of some sort, shot from water guns or buckets or fire hoses. I think the choice this year was milk and glue. Needless to say, I was very sad that I missed that one. That must have been a blast. (Get it?! BLAST! Eeeek! I'm sounding more and more like my father all the time.)

Then, of course, there is the football game itself. This is the centerpiece for all the Homecoming shenanigans and goings-on. Indeed, football is, for some reason, the all-encompassing essence of school spirit. Football in Texas can officially be categorized as a religion. If football is religion, then the Homecoming game is High Mass.

The wonderful thing about a Homecoming game is that it really doesn't matter whether your team wins. This is really important for Baylor University, because we haven't won a Homecoming game since disco went out of style. No, it's all about the event. In high school the important thing was the mum. If a girl didn't have a mum, she was socially shunned.

If a guy didn't get a girl a mum, he was automatically put on a blacklist by the girls and would not be permitted to get a date for the rest of his high school career. At our school these mums totally departed from nature. They'd have little bells and whistles and teddy bears stuck in the middle of them. The little gadgets weren't the only things, either. The real issue was the size. I swear some of these mums had to be flown in by helicopter and affixed with a welding torch. The poor girls who received these were usually immobilized until the mums could be removed.

I'm happy to report that in college, things are a lot different. Those silly mums are done away with. Instead, guys, you are expected to fly your dates to France, take them to a café to buy them a $300 salad and a pastry they won't eat. Of course, we needn't mention the fact that the girls are required to buy dresses that cost as much as their college education.

However, I'm not saying Homecoming and school spirit are all silliness. Au contraire, there is great good that can come of it. School spirit gives one a sense of belonging, and of taking pride in the fact that you're part of a group that is worth celebrating.

There is, of course, a major factor that will determine if and how much this notion of school spirit will affect you—your "Personal School Spirit Predisposition." In order for you to gauge your own PSSP, I have devised this little user-friendly contraption called the "Spirit-O-Meter." With it, all you have to do is answer some questions about yourself and you can see very easily how school spirit events will affect you.

Spirit-O-Meter

1. How familiar are you with your high school football team?

   A) I know the name, age, vital statistics, and birthplace of everyone on the football team.

   B) I go to the games sometimes. There are members of the opposite sex there.

   C) We have a football team?

2. How many items do you own with your school colors on them?

A) Plenty upon plenty. I never have to worry about matching. In fact, my undergarments have my school mascot on them.

B) One coffee cup and one long-sleeve shirt I bought by accident.

C) I am vaguely aware that my school has colors associated with it.

3. How many extracurricular activities have you taken part in during the past week?

A) Several dozen. Sometimes I catch myself singing "School days, school days, dear old Golden Rule days," without realizing it.

B) A couple. I emptied out my locker and checked out a book from the library. I'm in a writing club, or something.

C) I burned down my school and spat on
the ashes.

4. Do you love your school?

A) (Single tear rolling down cheek) Only
God and country come before it.

B) I dunno. It's all right, I guess.

C) What is love? Baby don't hurt me. Don't
hurt me. No more.

In order to check your score and see how you did, check
"Spirit-O-Meter Key"! I hope this helps you along your way
in your journey toward self-enlightenment. I'm only here
to help. God bless.

Spirit-O-Meter Key

If you answered all A's, you are truly
dedicated to your school. You will probably
never graduate—because leaving would break
your heart. Your best bet is to become a
teacher at your school, and be buried

underneath your classroom when you
pass away.

If you answered all B's, you are extremely
average. You will marry at an acceptable age,
have 2.5 kids, and live somewhere in middle-
class suburbia.

If you answered all C's, why are you a
student, anyway?

If you had mixed answers, I don't know what
to tell you. Obviously, you are confused.
Take the test again and again, until you
get consistent answers.

Thanksgiving

I was about to crack. I was just about to lose it. I was about
two and one-half days away from declaring myself legally
insane, and spending the rest of my life telling people that I
am a tea kettle. As fun, adventurous, and exciting as college is,
there comes a point where you just can't take it any more.
That point comes around mid-November. Fortunately the
Pilgrims were foresighted enough to have dinner with the
Indians around this time, so we get a week off from school.

Thanksgiving is a key time in the college freshman's life. It is
the first officially sanctioned "go home" time. For some of you,
this will be your first time to be back home since the summer.
To those of you who go home every weekend, this is just a very
long weekend with a very large meal.

Some of my earliest memories are of spending Thanksgiving
with my family. However, family probably has a little different
meaning to me than it does to the majority of you. My entire
immediate and extended family could all fit inside a closet. I

am an only child. My mom was an only child. My dad has one sister. She has an only child. You add my grandparents in and that's it. So we get none of this millions-of-people-running-around, "Home Alone" kind of thing.

Mine was a strange kind of homecoming. Once again, due to this new dual nature of home, I was leaving home to go "home." Once there, it seemed I was travelling back a year in time. All of us that had gone our separate ways were back again. We were a year older, but we didn't feel it, and we certainly didn't act it.

Maybe I should explain a little about the nature of my friends. My best friend is Spencer, whom I met when I was a freshman in high school. The first time I met him was at a birthday party. He was the hot item, of course, as he was the new boy and (so I've heard from reliable sources) quite the stud. I, of course, instantly disliked him on sight, because he got attention and I didn't. I refused to speak to him. My parents suggested that I get to know him, as I was going to be in high school with him—I disagreed.

As luck, or maybe it was God, would have it however, he and I were placed side by side in our theater class. The first couple of days we just stared at each other, but then I got tired of that and struck up a conversation with him. During the course of this conversation, I discovered he was a raving lunatic. This was a great discovery for me because, as you can probably tell, I do a fair share of raving myself. From that conversation sprang forth the best friendship I've ever had. From that day forward we were inseparable. Except, of course, for this whole college thing.

Not long after I met Spencer, I met Chris. Chris isn't so much a lunatic as he is a psycho. He, we discovered, is fond of talking very loudly all the time and shoving chicken sandwiches into people's eyes. Shortly after Chris came Andy, and the group was complete. I could write a book on Andy alone, but I think I can summarize him by saying he has a closet full of Star Wars action figures and a redhead fixation. When all four of us were together, nothing was safe. Coincidentally, the memories I have of them are the ones I cherish above all else.

We made movies. The first one we made was for the presentation aspect of a biology project. It was called *Dr. Fuher*. In the vein of *Jurassic Park*, we made a film about bioethics and what happens when you mix elephant, cheetah, and something else's DNA in a microwave. The result, according to the film, was something that looked like a potato with a thingy stuck into it. We made several other movies, including *Vote Carl Rogerson*, which followed the campaign of a presidential hopeful whose foreign policy was, "Nuke 'em." There was also an action/adventure/disaster movie called *Earthquake 2: The Remembrance*, in which a terrible catastrophe befalls the world and only some magical underwear saves the day.

The Bible says there are those rare friends who are closer than brothers, and I'm here to tell you that they're great. In fact, they're better than great. They are little vestiges of heaven on earth. Good heavens, I'm sounding sappy. But you know what? What's life if you don't get sappy about it every now and then? I'm pressing on, no apologies.

Now that I am in college, I look back at those memories, and a goofy smile comes to my face. A strange feeling overcomes me, which happens a lot these days. It is a bittersweet feeling. I loved the past. I loved it. I don't know that I will ever have more blissful, carefree, and just downright enjoyable days than I did in high school. From laughing with those I loved to crying on their shoulders and having them cry on mine—the experience as a whole is something I wouldn't trade for anything. The feeling doesn't end there. It's also a trembling for the future. Not trembling out of fear, but out of anticipation. I've had this little taste of life, freedom, and responsibility, and I'm chomping at the bit to get more of it.

I'm sure that many of you are saying (as you have been saying for the past few chapters), "This guy has lost his gourd. What does this have to do with Thanksgiving?" Well, I'll tell you. In my humble opinion, Thanksgiving, in the true sense, is or should be more than parades and football and lying around feeling like a beached whale. It should contain a spirit of gratitude for everything that has been put into our lives, and indeed, life itself.

The reason I am droning on and on about my friends and the times we've had is that I thank God every time I think of them. If you're reading this book, there's probably a lot that you can be thankful for. You're considering going off to college, or perhaps you're already there. This alone is a distinct privilege.

Plenty of folks do not and never will have that opportunity. Beyond that, the fact we live in a society allowing these kinds of dreams to become a reality is a blessing.

Also, be thankful for your parents. I know that for many of you, these relationships are defined by pain and disagreement. However, I doubt that you will find anyone who will love and support you more in the long run. Be thankful for the lessons they taught you. They will prove to be invaluable tools in the future.

Be thankful for your friends. The true ones. If you don't have any that you can cry with, get some immediately. This is not as easy as it sounds, I know. To make yourself totally vulnerable is a risky business. It opens you up to a world of hurt. Believe me, I've seen good relationships go wrong. It's not pretty. Not at all. However, I'd take the potential pain of a broken relationship over the bland nothing of never opening up, any day.

Be thankful for yourself. I have never met a person that, once I got to know him or her well, didn't amaze me. Trust me, there is something you can do that no one else can. College is the perfect time to discover what that thing is. For me, it was writing this book. I mean, believe it or not, I'm just this kid. A year ago if you would have told this kid that he would be an author, this kid would have laughed in your face. You're always capable of doing more than you think you can. Don't let your expectations of how life is going to be limit you to a smaller world.

Last, and most important of all, be thankful for God. It is impossible to comprehend how indebted we are to Him. I mean, we hear all the time in Sunday School about Jesus and how He died for your sins (which really is mind-boggling), but there is so much more that we don't even take into consideration. What do you think keeps the molecules in your body pasted where they are and prevents them from flying out into space? I'll give you a hint. It's a three-letter word that starts with a "G." Don't you think that with our behavior sometimes it would be just a heck of a lot easier to let those atoms fly?

If you look at it that way, every waking breath is a blessing, not something that's owed to us. Any opportunity that comes our way above and beyond that is from God's sheer graciousness. If you take a step back from our laughable lives and catch a glimpse of the larger picture, it's difficult to feel anything but gratitude. So there's something to feel thankful for. Let your first college Thanksgiving live up to its name.

It's the End of the Semester as We Know It

(And I Feel Fine...)

Well, I don't really know what to think. It crept up on me. Seemingly, only yesterday I was graduating from high school and everyone was taking pictures of me in that ridiculous robe and mortarboard get-up. Suddenly today I am home and finished with my first semester of college. I have completed entire courses. Eek.

The really scary thing with this whole ordeal is the dual nature of the time spent here. Although it seems like yesterday that I graduated from high school, it also seems like it's been years since I was living at home. I come back, and everything feels strange. Life has continued to evolve here despite my absence. I went to a theater party the other night. The group that used to be my family is now populated with people I don't know. Except for my closest friends, I feel like a stranger here at home.

I'm getting way ahead of myself. The end of the semester didn't sneak up on me totally unnoticed. The school wouldn't have allowed that. It would be uncollegiate. They have to put your brain through the meat grinder first. My religion professor was very kind to point out to us that no matter how well we had been doing in the class up to that point, the final exam counted for 40 percent of the final grade. Now, I don't know about you, but that worries me. I'm relatively good at taking exams, but there are days that I forget to bring my brain to class. On those days I am lucky if I can spell my name correctly given three tries. So basically what you have to do is pray that you don't have one of those days when you're supposed to take one of these giant bloodsucking exams.

Since I have spent the better part of my life playing some form of basketball, and I need to make an analogy here—I'm going to draw some parallels. The semester is kind of like a big basketball game. You start off on kind of unfamiliar territory, and don't really know who to pass the ball to, where to go, or perhaps even what team you're on. Then, as the game progresses and starts to get more cohesive, you begin to realize what you're supposed to be doing, and you scramble to start doing it, to make up for all the time you spent trying to figure out what to do.

Eventually you fall into a pattern and start to wonder why you thought the game was so difficult in the first place. That point is exactly when the collegiate staff decides to ruffle the collective feathers of the students, so to speak. As the air starts to grow colder (for those of us in Texas, this means it starts to dip below 80 degrees), you start to hear the word "finals" drifting into the air.

Everyone starts getting a little more anxious-looking. As it comes to the one-week mark, you see many of your fellow students with rings under their eyes. You hear stories such as, "Dude, I've stayed up for thirty-six consecutive hours studying for this exam." My big worry was this neat little theater course called "Costume Elements." The students taking this class, myself included, are required to sew various garments using a sewing machine. This is all fine and dandy until you take into account that I have the same innate sewing ability that God gave a South African petunia. As I have said before, any sewing project of mine I consider a success if I do not sew my fingers together. Generally when I am in the process of making my "garments" the class gathers around to watch me sew so they can laugh at me shamelessly.

This reaction from my fellow classmates has discouraged me from making a whole lot of "garments." No one likes to be laughed at, especially when one is in danger of sewing one's fingers together. The problem arose when I discovered, a few days before the end of the class, that you must complete all the garments assigned to you in order to pass the class. I thought this very bad news, since I had given up on sewing garments about two-and-one-half weeks after the class started.

Eventually it came down to my being forced to sew about six garments in forty-eight hours. A word to consumers: Garments made by Zach Arrington during the wee hours of the morning should not be viewed by small children, pregnant women, or persons with heart problems. Let's just say I was exploring that fine line that separates avant-garde clothing from a sheer unadulterated mess. Maybe I have invented some kind of "neo-ugly" look that will one day be wildly popular. Probably not, though.

By the end of the night I had created several items that, although almost totally indistinguishable from patches of moss, somehow counted as "garments," and I was saved. The other exams passed with equally smooth sailing. For an entire week I felt like I was getting ulcers all over the inside of my brain. Then suddenly it was over. I walked out of the building where I had taken the last exam and thought to myself, *Hey, that wasn't all that bad.* I guess I told myself that because human beings have a tendency to block pain from their memory. It's the same principal that gives women the ability to bear more than one child.

With a great sigh of relief the likes of which I have never sighed before, I went back to my dorm room and began packing my stuff. Unfortunately, every time I come home from school, I forget something vital. This time it was all of my bathroom supplies. Now I smell like a rat, and nobody wants to play with me. Maybe that's the reason I feel so out of place coming back here. I don't think so, though.

It's very strange to realize that life in your hometown goes merrily along its way without you. Sure there are tons of people here who remember me—and who I would still call friends—but they now have four months of life history that I haven't been a part of. Not to mention the four months of time that *I* have spent without *them*. Add that together and you get eight months of personal history from which you and your friends back home have been separated.

All of my friends still in high school now have plenty of inside jokes that I don't get. That's what really got me. You see, when I was there, I was present for the birth of just about every inside joke. I helped create most of them. If there was going to be somebody who didn't get it, it sure as Pete wasn't going to be me. Now they sit around laughing at experiences and things that I have no idea about. I just have to sit around all night going, "What? What? What was that? When did that happen?"

This is your brain on college. Any questions? I know I have plenty.

Couple this with trying to adjust to totally new surroundings at college, and it makes for a disheartening mix. Believe me, I'm not anywhere near adjusted. It's been really hard to find the kind of kindred spirits I had in high school. I think I've been living in denial for the past four months, thinking that my social life was just going to fix itself, and someday someone was going to come and knock on my door and say, "Hi, Zach, my name is Such and Such. I have noticed you from afar, and have decided that I want to be your new best friend. What do you say?"

Much to my disappointment, that hasn't happened yet. The more time that passes, and I sit at my desk alone, the more I start to think that it isn't going to happen. I haven't had to make good friends in at least four years. I've changed a lot in four years. Worse than that, I don't remember how I got the good friends I have now. Near as I can figure, we just all decided unanimously to become best friends one day.

Please don't let me get you thinking, however, that it's really that bad. Just like any other transition, there will be turbulence. That's to be expected. If moving from home to college was as difficult as outsmarting a tree, there would really be no need to write a book on it.

The Christmas vacation is a wonderful and necessary invention that lets you take a break from all this adjusting you've been having to do for the previous four months and breathe for a little bit. If you're anything like me, this is a good thing, because I was pretty close to running out of oxygen. Just hanging out with all my old buds is such a relief. It makes me happy. A beautiful aspect of college life is that Christmas break is a month long! Christmas hasn't been this much fun since I was seven.

So, hey, kick back, relax, come running downstairs in your cute pink foot-padded pajamas on Christmas morning.

Avoid getting run over by intoxicated maniacs on New Year's Eve, and come back to school refreshed and ready to give it the old college try once again. Oh, and remember to thank your grandparents for the money.

The Collegiate Style

Let me take you back to an especially joyful period of my life.
(Author's note: The previous sentence is dripping with
sarcasm.) The year was 1989, and I was in the third grade. I
didn't have a whole lot of really good friends in the third
grade. In fact, I was what most of the other kids called "kind of
strange." I played with imaginary people a lot. I talked to trees.
This kind of behavior generally doesn't allow you many social
privileges in the third grade. I was never even considered as a
candidate for sitting at the cool table. My Super Mario
lunchbox and I sat over in the corner.

My lack of social interaction was very evident during recess.
Every week a kid named Bill would have a new toy to play with
when the recess bell rang. Somehow Bill would go and find the
coolest toy in the entire toy store and purchase it—every week.
Then he would bring it to school each Monday and hold it up
for the world to inspect. The world would ooh and ahh,
mouths agape at the new item Bill had been so kind to grace
everybody's presence with. Of course, then everyone had to

have Bill's toy. By Wednesday there would be a little flock of boys on the tennis court playing with official Bill toys, or at least Bill-compatible toys.

I didn't have the luxury of going out and buying a new Bill toy every week. I had a Star Wars Y-Wing and a bunch of Legos. I had tried bringing these items to school, but it was made very clear to me that these were NOT Bill-compatible toys. So back to the trees it was for me. While the rest of the class was ambitiously trying to climb the social ladder of third grade, I was saving the universe from . . . uhh . . . trees.

I'm not sure whatever became of Bill. I left that school after fourth grade and have never seen him since. I'm sure he must be somewhere in *People* magazine's "America's 25 Most Intriguing People" section. If he's not there yet, he will be shortly. The reason I bring up Bill and my third grade escapades is that, in principle, things haven't changed all that much. College bears a whole lot of similarity to grade school. Sad as it may be, you are still labeled by the products you buy. In college, the only change is from the kinds of toys you buy to the kinds of clothes you wear, and the kind of music you listen to.

Believe me, at lunchtime, the cool table is back, and its influence is stronger than ever. Only now it has an official name. It's where the "Beta Gamma Gamma Epsilon Omega Alpha Charlie Seven One Niners" sit. (The names may vary, depending on the college.) At Baylor at least, the Greek clubs reign supreme.

However, the flip side of this issue is that since universities are huge, and contain such a diverse amount of people, you're almost always guaranteed to find people who share your likes and dislikes. If your cup of tea is the "Christian Ska Punkers Who Eat Cheeseburgers on Tuesdays Club," I'm sure you'll find the doors wide open. If there's not one on your campus, start one. You'll probably find people who want to join—whatever floats your bran muffin.

The only real problem with writing a chapter on the popular styles on a college campus is that by the time it is published, the styles I discuss will be utterly and completely outdated. Not only that, I'm the last person in the world I'd come to for fashion advice. One day, I was told the way I dress was "retro preppy cowboy funk" or something. If this is what my friends say about me, I'd hate to hear from someone who genuinely dislikes me.

In fact, the best advice I can give you on college style is to dress like yourself. If you feel like getting all prettied up and wowing everyone with your impeccable fashion know-how, then by golly you go get 'em. If someday you want to borrow my black shirt with fake snakeskin on the collar and sleeves, be my guest. Just don't blame me for the consequences.

I think the best way to go is variety. Don't lock yourself into any one style. Don't let Abercrombie & Fitch own your soul (please). Of course, on the flip side, don't wear feather boas to class every day. Wear something nice and normal just to keep them on their toes. That way, people don't lock you into a certain mold and categorize you without even knowing who you are. Most importantly: Don't try to fit into a certain category so much that you're willing to sacrifice your individuality. You're going to need that later.

The collegiate style is a lot different from the high school style, though. For high school, all you had to do was get dressed, make an appearance for a few hours, and then it was back home to your life. Here in the college world, everyone you go to school with lives within half a mile of you. School and home are one and the same. So generally, what you wear to class is what you wear during your "home" time.

The net result of all this, so I have been told, is that during the first part of each semester, everyone tries to impress everyone else and wears all the nice stuff, and spends an hour getting ready in the morning. Then about halfway through the semester, once the college fatigue starts to set in, people realize they could gain another half hour of sleep by not caring what they look like when they go into class. Maslow's hierarchy of needs sets in, and pretty soon all of the 8:00 classes start looking like "morning of the living dead." That is, if you happen to have the energy to look around and observe.

As I have said before, it is impossible for me to tell you what is "out" and what is "in" style-wise. This entire chapter is based on the assumption that you care in the first place. If you honestly don't care what you wear, and you can find a group of people who support you in this, then by all means go that route. That's probably the easiest one to take. I could probably spend the rest of my life walking around in my pajamas, but I just don't have the guts. If you do, then more power to you. You'll live in comfort for the rest of your days.

However, just for kicks, and so we can look back in thirty years and laugh at ourselves and our children can laugh at us, here is a brief look at what is in style on the college campus of today:

(A) Anything from Abercrombie & Fitch. This
    is a fine clothing store that has been

in business since 1892 and used to sell hunting gear to high-profile people like Teddy Roosevelt. A few years ago, A&F changed its marketing scheme. The modus operandi is now officially, "Hey, let's make advertisements targeting young Americans and mark all our products up to ridiculously high prices." I have no idea how they got that to fly, but if you ask me, those people are geniuses.

(B) Cargo pants with those neat little pocket thingies on the side. I think these things are great. I'm a big fan of random pockets. I have never seen anyone put anything in these pockets, and they serve no practical function. They look like military fatigues, but hey, we love 'em!

(C) Hats with the tops cut off so they look like visors. This is something I don't understand. I guess the underlying psychological meaning is something like, "Hey, I've got the financial stability to cut up my hat and wear it around."

And there are so many more. Go to your local college campus and look at all the goofy kids walking around. If you really want to be cool, look at what they're all wearing, and go out and buy the same thing. Congratulations. Now you're cool. The end.

Round Two ... Fight!

Well, as they say—and they are usually right—all good
things must come to an end. The Christmas break finally
wound down. Although now I'm not so sure that it's totally
a bad thing. Let it be known that three weeks is a long
time. This is the first time, in fact, that I have thought that
a break was long enough. I was able to get fully recharged.
This was mainly because I spent about twelve hours in bed
every night. And I got to see my friends again.

Christmastime spent laughing and sleeping does wonders
for the soul. I feel relaxed and refreshed and almost ready
to spend the next few months working non-stop on just six
and one-half hours of sleep each week. In fact, being back
at college has been great so far. Better than great. These
past few days have contained more joy than the entire
previous semester. I don't have to go around introducing
myself to the same people and having them introduce
themselves to me twenty-four hours a day. I kind of know
who my crowd is, and it's been a blast to get back with

them. I didn't realize what good friends I'd made until I left them all for three weeks.

I came back on a Sunday night, bringing a mountain of stuff with me. I don't know how common this is, but when I went home I realized just how much cool stuff I had left behind that would be really useful back at the dorm.

I packed up my dad's old stereo from his college days and a bunch of other random junk I thought I could either use or would just find interesting lying around the room. What I forgot to consider, though, was exactly how much space we don't have in the dorm. I guess I forgot about the whole sleeping on the CD case thing. So I arrived back at the dorm room with this obscenely huge pile of stuff, and dumped it all on the floor.

I thought my roommates, when they saw the neat treasury of stuff that I had brought back to share with them, would say "Hey Zach, that's great! Thanks for thoughtfully amassing this great treasury of wonderful random things to share with us. We appreciate you. Group hug." Instead, when I dumped my wonderful treasury of random things on the floor, they gave me this look that said, "Ah, welcome back from the Christmas break. Obviously you have flushed your brain down the toilet. Clean that up immediately."

They were right. So far we have not found a way to store the wonderful treasury of random things I fondly refer to as the "mess." So now, day in and day out, we live with this wonderful mess that exists where our floor used to be. But at least it's a very interesting mess. It's my mess.

There was a shocking difference between the first day of classes this semester versus last semester. When you go to college for the first time, it's a shockingly big deal. Your life smacks you in the face with the grace of a truckload of concrete marmots and says, "G'day mate (yes, for the sake of this illustration, you are Australian); you are in COLLEGE now. There's no two ways about it, mate. It's good on ya, but you're a college person now, and you'd better bloody well cope."

Entering the second semester, although all the classes are new and you're still a little disoriented, your mind thinks, *Oh, I'm back here again.* And so you are. In some of the classes there may be familiar faces, which is certainly a change from the previous semester. Walking into my astronomy class, I looked around and was surprised to be able to say to myself, *Hey, there's So and So, and over there is Such and Such, and Whozit-Sniggly!*

Another observation—the campus seems·to be a lot smaller now. This is definitely a good thing, because when you first get to a college campus·and compare it to high school, it threatens to eat you whole. They make it confusing on purpose. In high school, if there are separate buildings on campus, they are called by an appropriate name. If there is a certain building in high school that contains, say, a bunch of science classrooms and some labs, it's called "the Science Building." At college, the same building would not be called "the Science Building." It would be named "the Herbert Schmelding W.J. Griffin-Bubbly Scientorium." Instead of having the word "science" anywhere on your schedule to give you some sort of clue, you get "HSWJBGS Rm. 314." Then, I guess as a test to see if you have the wits to be a real college student, you get to figure out all on your own what "HSWJBGS" means.

Generally, I have discovered that those students who make it to their second semester of college are more concerned about their grades than they were during the first semester. (By the way, I always get the word semester confused with trimester. The second semester is something entirely different than the second trimester. Keep that in mind.) Anyway, the point is that kids generally strive harder for good grades during the second semester. The reason for this, especially at Baylor, where transcripts are sent home and opened by parents without any editing, is that college students are forced to be accountable for their grades.

It seems the grades received by college students during their first semester are almost always lower than expected, except for those who know for a fact that they got a 4.0 because they have never missed a test question in their lives. You people make me sick—in a good sort of way. I suppose that society needs your kind around. If we didn't have you, why then we'd be fresh out of lawyers and doctors and corporate executives. Then all the lawyer and doctor and corporate executive positions would have to be filled by people like me, in which case the entire universe would immediately self-destruct.

So now there is much studying going on, but also some socializing and general clowning around. These are the three main components of college life. They finally take hold during the second semester because you are finally able to "settle down" and establish a set of actions that you can dub "a routine." These three components of college life replace the three main components of high school life, which were eating, sleeping, and disagreeing with your parents. Eating, as has been discussed before, is still a moderately important part of college life, and probably falls fourth or fifth on the list. Sleeping takes a backseat to pretty much everything else, and is on the priority list just below belly button hygiene.

The third essential element of high school life— disagreeing with your parents—does not disappear, but changes dynamics dramatically. You see, when you are living with your parents at home, oftentimes you view them as a burden. They put limits on you, make seemingly irrational decisions, and impose restrictions on what, from your perspective, would otherwise be a perfectly happy and carefree life. When you get to college, the dynamics change because, unless you are going on some kind of full-ride scholarship, your parents have a rope around your neck in one hand and a fistful of dollars in the other. This generally leads people to treat the folks with more respect.

To review then: Compared to when I first arrived on campus, I like this semester just a whole piggy piggy bunch more. You return to campus and have a general (even if slightly deranged) idea of what's going on in the bright bustling university world around you.

There are enough consistencies now so you can have a "normal" day instead of every day being an unpredictable adventure filled with things that have no meaning to you. Fortunately, this coin has two good sides. Despite the fact that you have the world a bit more in perspective now, you're still a freshman, and being in college still hasn't quite lost that ethereal wonder. You still have your new life to enjoy. I'm going to go find a way to revel in mine now.

Things You Didn't Have to Do Before

Hungry, Hungry Dryer

"Where are your socks?"

I have a pink shirt. I do not have a pink shirt because I bought a pink shirt. It is in my possession because I made it. I did not intend to make it. Oh, no. I would have been perfectly happy without a pink shirt. Pink shirts aren't exactly the going fashion for college-age males. My life was better without this pink shirt.

Let me explain why this pink shirt is such a big deal and why it is pertinent to this chapter. Once upon a time, I was on the freshman basketball team at Tomball High School. I didn't start, but I was the sixth man, coming off the bench quite often to replace the starters. And we were good. We were REALLY good. In fact, that year we never lost a game. We went twenty-four and zero. This is a feat that has not been equaled before or since at that high school, or any other schools in the district. Needless to say, this is a time of great nostalgia for me. I look back on this time quite fondly, and any items associated with it are of great importance.

Every one of us who was on that team had a warm-up shirt we wore to every game and used (amazingly) to warm up. It was a white shirt with our last names and jersey numbers written on it in red. Red and white were our school colors, you see. If you remember your kindergarten science, you will recall that when you mix the colors red and white together, you get a new color: pink. This effect is quite evident when one does not know how to operate a washing machine properly. The red combines with the white, and it makes the whole thing (sob) pink.

In fact, if you're really lucky, and your washing machine is ornery enough, you can get an entire wash load of pink items. Just one good red towel is enough to give you dozens of pink socks, pink T-shirts, little pink undies (my favorite), and pink sweatpants. Yes, my friends, washing your own clothes is one of the hideous monsters you will have to face alone when you go off to college.

In case your mother didn't go over the basics with you, and you're standing there with a load of wash that you haven't the foggiest idea how to manage, I'll tell you what I remember of the basic steps of clothes-washing.

Step One: Separate all your clothes into piles. This may seem like it's going to be smooth sailing at first, but to the ADD child like me, staying focused on the project at hand in order not to end up with the dreaded pink clothing items is indeed a daunting task.

Your clothes need to be separated according to a couple of determining factors. The first is what kind of material your clothes are made of. Knits, which are your T-shirts and things of that sort, should be separated from the rest. Then there are your permanent press things, which include khakis, jeans, and nice shirts. Then you have your towels. You get the picture.

If you have questions about what kind of material your things are made of, look on the tag. That will generally tell you. Or, this could provide a good excuse to call your mother. Moms start to complain if you don't do that. You could knock out two birds with one stone.

Find out what kind of material your laundry is, and make your mother happy. It's that simple. Strange thing about mothers: When you go off to college, they will call you and ask you something asinine like "How was your day?" Because you don't live at home anymore, you don't have the privilege of just saying "fine." I find myself getting into long discussions about what went on that day. Strange.

Anyway, back to laundry: Once you've created separate laundry piles based on fabric, you need to sort according to color. This is a somewhat easier task, as even the untrained eye can tell a red shirt from a white shirt. This is much, much easier than distinguishing a knit shirt from a whatever-else shirt. Now that you have nobly divided your clothes into separate piles, it is time to venture further into the unknown—be brave.

Step Two: Find a washing machine. If you were raised like some friends of mine, you will need someone to point one out, as you have never done a lick of laundry in your pampered lives. The trick about most college washing machines is that unlike the ones that Mom ran, these are entrepreneurial. They require you to make a deposit of cash money before they will let you make use of their services. This is especially disconcerting when one has completely run out of cash money, and must wear one's kindergarten graduation T-shirt and a pair of jams until one receives more cash money.

When God, on the eighth day, made washing machines, He said this: "Thou shalt wash thy darkest clothing items in the cool water. Thou shalt wash thy lighter clothing items, including thy pastel ones, in the warm water. Thou shalt not mix the light clothing with the dark clothing. If thou mixeth the dark with the light, then I, the Lord thy God, shall become wrathful and send Satan, the 'prince of pink clothing,' directly into thy washing machine, and he shall wreak much havoc, and all thy friends shall laugh at thee."

Heed well those words. They will save you much embarrassment at the hands of thy friends. Every washing machine (at least those in America—I don't know about those metric countries) will generally have a setting that corresponds with the type of material you are washing ("knits" for knits, and so on). Now that you have acquired all this knowledge, all that is left to do is twist the knobs and pull the thingies, and *voila!* you have a load of freshly washed clothes.

The only major problem with your freshly washed clothes (assuming, of course, that Satan didn't make a guest appearance in your washing machine and destroy them), is that they are all soaking wet. Society, in its infinite wisdom, has devised a contraption to help you solve this problem. The "dryer!" Dun dun dun DUN! (Fanfare courtesy of the London Symphony Orchestra.) The trouble, once again, with college dryers is that they also require an up-front advance of cash money. I find that it is nice to have a big jar of quarters lying around for these occasions (and for those occasions when you want to annoy the employees of restaurants by insisting that you have nothing larger to pay with).

Step Three: Drying your clothes. You'll want to put your permanent press items in there on high heat, since they're generally made of sterner stuff. Counterwise (I made up another word. Hey, Shakespeare did it, so can I. Says so in the Constitution), your knits should be dried on low heat. The reason for this is they are made of the fabric of our lives (cotton), and they will shrink. This is great for those of you who can wear tight clothes without shame. This category of people does not include me. The state of Texas has put a restraining order against me, compelling me to stay at least five yards away from any item of Spandex clothing.

Some college dryers, including the marvelous specimens at Baylor University, take their sweet time drying your clothes. It is not uncommon for you to have to run your clothes through them two or three times. Of course, you have to pay each time—it's capitalism at its worst.

Barring any serious accident, whenever the little dryer bell dings, your wash should be done. All that remains now is to go back and throw all your freshly cleaned clothes on the floor of your room where they belong. Then you get to go back and do it again in a week. (Or, if you have a good supply of those kindergarten T-shirts, six weeks.)

There are, of course, many other areas of your life that you will have to attend to now that you haven't had to before, such as getting your hair cut, making sure your car (should you have one) is up and running, and taking yourself to the doctor if one of your limbs falls off. Unfortunately, up to this point I've been too chicken to do any of these things away from home. If the car needs work, if I need a haircut, if there is generally anything important that needs to be done, I go home to do it.

Perhaps in the future I will be brave enough of spirit to venture out into the wilds of Waco and try to fend for myself. When I do, you can be sure there will be a sequel to this chapter, splendid and written in full glory. Until such time, I bid you goodnight. I must go to sleep and get up for class, and I have only a little less than six hours in which to do it.

P.S. Why is it called, "Going to sleep?" You're not going anywhere. You're just falling asleep. Of course, falling doesn't make that much sense either. Goodness, what a silly language we have here. Someone ought to complain. Write your congressman. It's late. Goodnight.

Chapter
Eighteen

Ye Good Olde College Towne

> —— Welcome to ——
>
> ## Your College Town
>
> Pop. Plenty
>
> "Abandon hope, all ye who enter here."

Waco, Texas. It's all about local flavor. During my stint here at Baylor University, I have come to realize that the city (or lack thereof) in which your university is located will affect the kind of college experience you have. As self-contained as a campus may be, a college located in the heart of New York City is going to have a fundamentally different feel than a college in Tumbleweeds, Wyoming. My quest for the best (affordable) college took me through all kinds of college towns, from the meager to the monstrous.

Houston, my native city, is just about as monstrous as they come. It is spread out over roughly half the state of Texas. Plenty of people in the Houston area need to go to college. Thus, the University of Houston is composed mainly of people who live in Houston and commute to the university just as they would to a high school. The result is there is very little social interaction among the people who attend the university. (I have this on good authority from people who attend there.)

Basically you just slip through the door in the morning, maybe say hello to the class in general if you're feeling chipper, take your seat, and learn. When you are done learning for the day, you gather your things and find the nearest exit. Then you go home, and everything's good.

On the other hand, I also have a friend who attends John Brown University in Armpit, Arkansas. It's a small campus out in the middle of chicken wire and outhouse country. Within about half a semester, you know everyone you want to know, dislike everyone you want to dislike, and you know exactly where you're going to stand socially for the next three and one-half years.

Then you have monstrous schools in semi-monstrous cities. UT (The University of Texas) is a good example. It has an enrollment that accounts for a relatively large percentage of Austin's population. I think it holds about 50,000 of the roughly 600,000 people in the city. Austin is the capital of Texas, and there are a goodly number of respectable people living in the area. Thus Austin retains its own character as a city, but one that is very conducive for college life.

When your college accounts for a third or half of the population of a town, then you are officially living in a college town. The aptly named College Station is a good example, for it is the home of Texas A&M. That college runs that town. The town caters to the college's needs, and the college loves it.

To give an example of the kinds of things you will run across in your college town, I shall take Waco as an example, the ever so humble home of Baylor University, and dissect it for your educational betterment, or something. My first visit to Waco was for the sole purpose of checking out Baylor. We drove in at night. On this particular night there happened to be a major astronomical event in which all of the planets lined up in alphabetical order. As I looked out my window and saw all the little planets lined up right in front of the moon, I remember thinking, *You know, ancient peoples would have regarded this as a sign or something. Especially if they were on the eve of making a life-changing decision, as I am.* Call it fate, providence, or whatever you like.

Now that I look back on that coincidence, I don't really regard it as strange at all. It seems to fit the pattern of the way things work around here. If I have learned anything about this area during my time at Baylor it is this: Kooky things happen in Waco. These are not necessarily bad things, they are just quirky things. You just see them and say "Okay" and walk on.

From what I have heard, Waco started out as a quickly growing city. It was supposed to be another Houston or Dallas. Businesses were flocking to the downtown area, which is nestled in a valley on the banks of the Brazos River. (This is actually a very pretty sight when the river isn't down 80 feet because of drought.) Waco was the first city in Texas (so I hear) to construct a skyscraper. It is called the ALICO building, and it was apparently the marvel of its time. Constructed of concrete with smallish windows running up to the top, where an American flag was proudly flown next to a Texas flag, the ALICO building towered over its little metropolis in style. Plans were being drawn to bring more businesses in and create another booming city.

However, Mother Nature, in order that her view of the Brazos
River wouldn't be obstructed, decided that it was a good time
to run a tornado right through the middle of downtown.
It destroyed, completely or partially, every building in
the downtown vicinity, except, of course, our beloved
ALICO building.

The result: To this day, the downtown area of Waco is mapped
out like a major metropolis, with really wide one-way streets,
only there's nothing lining them except little parks and retail
stores with the occasional commercial building. In the middle
if it all, standing proud and tall, is the ALICO building,
straight out of the late-nineteenth century.

All in all, it presents an environment that is very . . . I'll say
interesting. As I said at the beginning, it's all about local flavor.
Waco has, like most college towns I've encountered, a main
strip that contains movie theaters, restaurants, and enterprises
for general entertainment. Of course, it contains the one
feature that no city-raised college kid can live without for
long—a mall.

There is always but always a "mall" within shouting distance of
a major college. The reason I say "mall" with quotation marks
is that sometimes these enterprises are not the malls we are

used to. In my college travels, I visited Steven F. Austin State University. It is a pretty campus nestled within the majestic pine trees of Nacogdoches, Texas (fondly referred to as NacoNowhere). When I inquired, the people there were very proud to say that Nacogdoches indeed had a mall, and that I was invited to go check it out. We drove about ten minutes away from the campus, only to discover that their "mall" was in fact something like a JC Penney and a Marshall's linked together by an ice cream shop and a water fountain.

In Waco, there are several interesting little oddities. These include the overabundance of Wal-Marts. In a town of little more than 100,000, who would have thought that you would need four or five Wal-Mart Supercenters within a 15-mile radius? There is also the road behind the college that, for the length of about two miles, features businesses that manufacture gravestones. Not just one gravestone business, but several of them. Thus, for two miles, the road is lined with unmarked gravestones. This can be quite unsettling when one does not know where one is, and one is just trying to find the cleaners.

Of course the whole David Koresh thing goes without mentioning. Literally. (The locals have blocked it out of their memory and probably wouldn't know what you were talking about if you asked them.)

So indeed, you should be sure to check out the local surroundings before you make the final decision for college. For those of you who are reading this book and are already enrolled at college, too bad. You should have waited for the release of this book before making such a crucial decision. Shame on you.

However, regardless of which college you go to, whether it be out in the boondocks, or smack dab in the heart of a bustling city, some elements will remain constant. The first and foremost of these is the little ring of fast-food restaurants and convenience stores that are just a stone's throw away from campus. Mixed in with these are the gas stations that say they proudly support _____ (fill in name of the college), and then charge you a firstborn son for every gallon of gas.

Then, just outside that, generally you're going to have your movie theaters and finer restaurants, such as Friday's and Red Lobster. (Hey, for us college kids, this is *la crème de la crop*.) Many colleges will have what is called "the strip." This is usually a road with a bunch of stores and entertainment venues that appeal to the college-age crowd. These range in size and style depending on the college that supports them.

Despite the lengths I have gone to demonstrate how the local environment affects your college experience, don't let me scare you away from any college you like just because of what's around it. The most important things you need to look for are all located on the college campus. In the end, that should be your criteria for choosing. It's just that eventually, when you're on campus, you're going to look around and say, "You know, I've seen these buildings a million times. I need to get out and see the town." I endorse this. I do it myself. If you're ever in Waco, make sure to check out the two miles of gravestones.

Ouch!

Here is the sad but true tale of one Zach Arrington, a key player on the Baylor University Theater "Flying BUTs." An explanation: Since the anagram of Baylor University Theater is BUT, the theater department has a field day with it. Because of this, anything that has to do with the department is in some way expressed using BUT. Thus the aerobic workout for theater majors becomes "Tight BUTs." Not to miss out on the fun, the Baylor University Theater intramural basketball team was dubbed the "Flying BUTs."

As you may know, "theater people" aren't usually thought to be the kind of people who play aggressive sports, especially in a competitive setting. This is true for the most part. However, because of some fluke, on the Baylor University Theater Flying BUTs all of the starting lineup of the team and even some of the bench players played varsity basketball for their high school.

Opponents came expecting to see a scraggly bunch of artsy-fartsy scrubs, but instead found some guys who actually knew

how to play a little ball. You'll have to forgive my gloating—
I'm just proud of us boys. So, to make a long story short, we
were the dark horses of the league. We lost only one "regular
season" game, and were invited to participate in the playoffs,
which, strangely enough, had never occurred to a theater
team before.

Not only were we invited to the playoffs, we won the first game
decisively. That was a Tuesday afternoon. The next round of
the playoffs was that evening. We all made plans to attend and
whip some intramural rear. I even made arrangements with
my director to get out of rehearsals early, which generally,
barring your own death, doesn't happen.

I arrived at the gym with plenty of time to dress and warm up
for what looked to be a very promising game. The warm-ups
went exceptionally well, with each side having its loyal band
of girlfriends cheering it on. It neared game time, and the
tension in the air increased dramatically. I have no idea why,
but for some reason, fraternity skins crawl at the thought of
getting spanked by a theater team. Oh well. Pride cometh
before a fall...

I controlled the opening tip-off and slapped the ball to our
point guard, who set us up and took us down court. I got

the ball at about the three-point line, and saw for some odd reason, there was nobody between me and the basket. I decided to kick off the night strong and take it in with much pizzazz. As I charged toward the hoop, a couple of their team members remembered they were supposed to be playing defense and decided it would be in their best interest to stop me.

The fact that I was going forward at an alarming rate and there were two very large entities coming at me forced me to take one of the strangest looking shots in human history. As soon as I let the ball go, I decided to focus all of my energies on landing my now-airborne body. Problems arose, however, when I looked down where the floor should have been and the only thing I saw was someone else's hand. In fact, that someone else's hand was the only thing I could see, except for one little patch of green, which didn't help me at all. So I just closed my eyes and hoped for the best.

Unfortunately, the best didn't happen. I landed on my feet, which was a good thing. What was not a good thing was that as I landed on my feet, my left knee locked. I bounced once, and on the second landing, my left knee bent backwards, and I heard this sound like someone was breaking a sausage with a hammer.

Not very long after that, I recognized I was in a great deal of pain. I reminded myself that this was a good thing, because it meant I wasn't going to have to spend the rest of my life writing with my teeth. By now there was the usual small crowd of people looking and hoping that you're just going to be able to get up and shake it off. I had no idea if my leg had fallen completely off, or if there were bones sticking out or what. It was at this point that I opened my mouth for the first time, and proved to myself forever and beyond a doubt that I am a guy.

"Did it go in?"

I didn't ask, "Am I going to be all right?" or "If I die, will you tell my parents I love them?" The state of my leg, or whether I would ever walk again, at that moment, was nowhere near as important as knowing whether I had succeeded in putting a sphere through a circle.

"Yes, Zach, it went in."

As far as I was concerned at that point, whatever injury I may have suffered was worth it if I had made the basket. Even if I died right there on the basketball court, at least it would be with honor. They could carve "He made the shot" on my gravestone for all I cared.

I decided then to direct my attention back to my leg and the agony it was putting me through. Then I started yelling and hitting the ground.

It was very obvious from the get-go that I wasn't going back in that game. I tried to put some weight on it. This solicited screams of "What in the periodic table do you think you're DOING?!" from all of the working tendons in my left knee (both of them). The rest of the evening was kind of a haze. I was dimly aware of the fact that our team lost by five points, and had I been in there, there's a good chance we might have won. That didn't make me feel any better.

I went home and tried to get some sleep. I couldn't. There was no possible comfortable position. I decided to watch a movie. I put in *The Shawshank Redemption*. This is a movie about people in prison beating the snot out of each other. It didn't help me get to sleep. I woke up the next morning and found that my desire to keep my leg immobile greatly outweighed my desire to go to class.

So I sat there, listening to the same CD over and over again because it just wasn't worth the effort to get up and get a new one. By far the worst thing about being sick or injured at college is the lack of pampering. When you're at home and you're sick or injured, you have the world at your fingertips. Especially when you're injured, because then you can eat whatever you like, and your mother is dying to cook it for you. At college all you get are your roommates bouncing around your room and enjoying their perfect health.

However, college misfortune is not totally without benefits. At Baylor University, there are at least a couple thousand very attractive girls who are studying pre-med because of their desire to help people who are in pain. I, ever the opportunist, dragged myself, pain and all, into the lobby of the girls dorm. Sure it was a cheap trick, but what can I say? I love sympathy.

Eventually I was persuaded to seek professional help (of the medical kind). My friend Rhett, who gets the Nobel Prize for "dragging Zach around while he's wounded," took me to the campus medical center. Now let me tell you something about myself. I don't know why this is (I suspect that it has something to do with the only-child syndrome), but I hate dealing with people I don't know. Despite being something of an extrovert, it scares me to death. I don't even like ordering fast food. So when it comes to entrusting my busted leg to complete strangers, you must know that I'm a little hesitant. Anyway, I was finally carted to the medical center, resolved to meet my fate.

To my pleasant surprise, the whole ordeal was pretty easily dealt with. All they did was swipe my student ID, and charge the expenses to my student account. Then all that's left is to wait in the antechamber for about six and one-half days and let the doctor tell you what's wrong with you. As it turns out, it was a sprained MCL. They gave me a brace, some crutches and a bottle of anti-inflammatories. It's almost a week later, and my leg is doing much better. Thanks for asking.

For those of you with a bad case of the homesickness bug, the first college sickness or injury may prove to be a daunting experience. That family support you're used to at home will have to be provided by friends at college. For me, at least, it really deepens the friendships you have. Because of these kinds of incidents, you're not allowed to stay on a surface level anymore. You're lying there broken and busted, and you must trust yourself to the hands of someone you may not have known for all that long. It's pretty darn efficient at breaking down walls.

Well, I'm proud to say that I emerged from my first major
college health run-in all right. In less than a couple of weeks
I'll be ready to go back out on those basketball courts so
I can break something else.

Chapter
Twenty

Roommates. Heh Heh.

If you have grown up in what most Americans would traditionally consider "normal" circumstances, for most of your life you have been living with at least one parent or legal guardian, and perhaps some siblings. People you know, people who are related to you. Like just about everything else in life, that changes when you get to college. Suddenly you are thrown into a living situation with people you may never have met before in your life—and when you meet them, you might wish you never had.

When I started the year, I didn't know my two roommates from Adam. One of them, Justin, is from Sweetwater, Texas. The other one, Bart, is from Dallas and is the son of a former Dallas Cowboy. I was the third wheel. Throw me in any long-term social situation and it automatically becomes interesting. Not always "good interesting," but definitely interesting.

I must admit when I first shipped off to college, I fell into a funk. I was used to having fun with a certain bunch of people, and I didn't know how to have fun with new people. Another thing that got in the way of forming good new relationships was that even among new people I acted as if I were in the presence of my old friends, which is to say, like a total lunatic.

These factors combined to create a rift between myself and my new roommates, and the events of those first few weeks affected my life from then on. To me, my roommates simply became strangers who shared the room with me. Not too long after that, they started making friends with all the other people on the hall, and having all their friends into the room all the time, which caused me to become even more estranged. This wasn't because having people in the room bothered me. On the contrary, I love people, and I like having them cramped in close quarters as often as possible. It was simply because I didn't know anyone to bring along so that I could show my roommates, "Look, I have friends too, see?"

Halfway through the first semester, Bart decided that it was time to bail. Even if you have perfectly ideal people for roommates (and at that point I was being anything but ideal), any time you have three people in a room barely big enough for two people, there's going to be trouble. And Bart decided that he had had enough trouble. So that left Justin and me in the room together.

That's when things started to pick up a little bit. They didn't improve by leaps and bounds, but I stopped dreading going home after school. (What a change from elementary school, eh?) I actually started talking to him in sentences longer than two words, and he started responding with real English words. I began to finally understand that even if I didn't know them from Adam, roommates aren't necessarily evil. About the time I realized this, another guy decided that he'd move in. His name is Griff and he's sitting about 8 feet to my right at this moment.

I really can't stress enough how important it is that you room with someone of similar moral standards. You can get over just about anything else. Annoying music can be put into headphones. If they decide to put pink flamingos up on the window, I can't say that necessarily you'll ever like it, but eventually you learn to cope. However, when it comes to clashing views of what's morally right and wrong, things can get ugly.

This, of course, goes for guys and girls alike. In fact, although I don't know all that much about women, I understand that girls with differing opinions are less likely to get along with each other than guys are. Kristen, whom you've heard from earlier, says she is kept awake nightly by hearing her next-door neighbors scream about something or other. Guys, unless things get really bad, are sometimes able to put it off and just say "whatever." Girls, with their eyes ever turned toward detail, will eliminate a roommate they dislike within the first couple of weeks. I guess it's one of those things about being from Venus.

So anyhoo, my roommates and I now exist in perfect harmony (not). But we're working on it. For the last little bit, I've been so busy with theater, and Justin busy with rushing one of those fraternities, that the room has just been a place to conduct business and sleep. However, it seems that the clouds have been lifted for me, and besides the dreaded hairdryer at 7:00 in the morning when I don't have class until 9:30, we seem to be getting along relatively well.

The best advice I can offer you is to get started on a good foot. Don't default on the first couple of weeks, because you will get irrevocably behind socially. I still don't know half the people that Justin or Griff knows. They get phone calls all the time, and very rarely, it seems to me, is it the same person. I'm doing well if I get a message and it's not from my mom. So I guess what I'm trying to say is this: Do absolutely everything you can to make your roommates your friends.

This is all assuming, of course, that you like people in general, and you don't see yourself wanting to become a mad hermit in the near future. I am an admitted extrovert, even though I'm not exceptionally good at meeting new people. This makes a bad combination because it means that I'm content to stick with the old people all the time. Once again, as good as the old people are, they're not here; only new people are. Roommates represent the new people that you will be spending the most time with over the coming year. These are people you are going to trust not to torment you in your sleep, or tie you up and rob you blind in the middle of the night.

I must warn you right now, though, that there is a curse on roommates. Especially if you're like me, and are not used to living with unrelated people. That curse? Even if your roommate is your best friend in the whole world, you will find several things about your roommate that just irritates the penguins out of you. Mark my words on this. Find any two people who have spent more than a month in a living situation together and they will have a long list of things about one another that agitate them regularly. Unless, of course, I'm that roommate, in which case, they will never have anything to complain about, seeing as how I am a perfect person all in all.

Visual illustration of someone getting the penguins annoyed out of him.

You have heard me mention my best friends from back home (Andy and Spencer) before. They decided it would be a good idea to room together. I knew from the onset that no good could come of this. These two guys, even though compatible in moral views, have totally incompatible living styles.

To appreciate this, you need to be acquainted with their upbringing. I have gone over to Spencer's house on many occasions and found him sitting in bed with the covers over his face, playing good old eight-bit Nintendo. This wouldn't seem so unusual except that when I go over it's usually 5:00 in the afternoon and he still hasn't left his bed. (Unless it's a school day, in which case, he goes back to sleep as soon as he

gets home.) He cleans his room very religiously. Every
Christmas and Easter.

On the other hand, Andy was raised by his mother. He gets
mad if you sit on his bed because it gets wrinkled. He doesn't
let you try to make amends and fix it yourself, because you
don't make it using the Andy method. The Andy method is, of
course, possible to follow properly only if you are Andy. So in
Andy's opinion, when it comes to the art of housekeeping,
Spencer falls terribly short of the mark.

It eventually came to the point where Andy went home and
got some masking tape. With this masking tape he roped off
certain sections and declared them "Andy territory." Andy
territory must not contain any of Spencer's mess. Any
violation of this rule results in Spencer getting an Andy lecture
on what an incredible slob he is. These speeches and his
constant habit of cleaning have led Spencer to dub Andy
"Little Missus." This title has led Andy to dub Spencer some
things that are not printable in this book.

So you see, it is very easy for your roommate situation to
quickly degenerate. I do not, however, want to make it seem
like your roommate, no matter who he or she is, will
automatically turn into the devil as soon as you move in

together. It is actually possible, so I have heard, to turn your roommates into your best friends. I wish I had more advice to dispense on this subject. But I've been given the opportunity to let you folks know what's up, so by golly, I'm going to do the best rootin'-tootin' fresh n' fruity job that I can. I just hope that you can garner some small nuggets of wisdom from my mistakes so you can avoid the same pitfalls.

I suppose the best I can offer is this: If there are days when you are angry with your roommate, just imagine if somebody cloned you and made you live with yourself. This thought should motivate you to forgive your roommate for his or her sins. Unless, of course, you are perfect. In that case, room with me.

Stress

(Eeeeeeeeeee...)

What stress looks like under a microscope.

During the last few weeks I have become very familiar with a phenomenon I didn't encounter much in high school. This, as you may have guessed from the chapter title, is stress. I do not mean to say I have never experienced stress. There were many nights when I had basketball practice and theater rehearsal back to back, the result being I went to school at 7:30 and didn't get home until after 10:00. There were fair amounts of stress there, to be sure. However, when one gets to college, stress changes dynamics a little bit.

Let's say that in high school you had a bunch of tests and practice for various activities, and a million little things were due the next day. When you came home, your parents would be there to make sure you were organized and were doing what you were supposed to be doing. (At least my parents did. Boy did they ever make sure.) I have said it before, and I'll say it again, when you are taken off to college, your parents are effectively removed from the responsibility radar. IT'S ALL UP TO YOU. (Stressed out yet?)

Now, if you're anything like me, you can find that notion more than a little distressing. I have a plan for combating stress that can end up being counterproductive. If things get too hot in the kitchen, I always have this urge to leave. This is a bad thing because generally by the time I remember that I am supposed to be back in the metaphorical kitchen, the kitchen is already metaphorically burning down, and it takes 100 times the effort to keep my life under some semblance of control.

The net result of this whole thing is what psychologists like to call stress. Webster defines stress as "stress, n. 1. emphasis. 2. difficulties. 3. a force causing strain." Now I don't know about the first one, but I'll wholeheartedly stand behind the second two. During the past two and one-half weeks, I have been busy straight from 9:00 in the morning until 11:00 at night. My particular case was with theater rehearsal. However, don't think a schedule like that only affects people who have things they have to practice, such as theater and music majors. I cringe to hear what kinds of tortures the business, psychology, and pre-med majors have to put up with. Not to mention those who rush any kind of Greek institution.

Let me describe to you what college stress feels like. It starts very subtly. You're sitting around your room one day, looking at all of your syllabi and thinking, "Gee, I sure signed up for a lot of things this semester." But then you remember that you're a competent and self-sufficient individual, and that you signed up for all this stuff because you can take it, and you'll be grateful for it all in the end. Then you enter into the joyous carefree period in which nothing is due for a while. You don't even see the tidal wave coming.

Then, one by one, the deadlines start creeping up on you. They are very skilled hunters, these deadlines. The real danger, if you remember, comes from the fact that they hunt in packs. This means that at first you have a few weeks of sunny days in which you don't have to worry about anything. Then one idle

Tuesday, you're sitting in your first class, and your professor very gently says, "Oh, and remember that such and such is due in a week." And you think, *Oh my! I'd forgotten all about that. No bother, though, I've still got a week to do it, and it's just one assignment, so that gives me all the time I need.*

After that class you pack up all your stuff, head to the next class, and sit down. Then this professor says, "Dear students, don't forget that this and that is due in a week." At this point stress starts to slip its tendrils around the fringes of your mind when you think, *This and that?! It's due next week, too?! That means I have to do both such and such AND this and that.*

Two days later, you realize that you need to complete such and such, this, that, and the other thing, plus two dozen other very important assignments, along with any extracurricular activities you have signed up to do in your "free time." At this point, stress feels like this: You look at all the stuff you have yet to do, and you lie down and try to die right there. When you realize that you can't get out of it that easily, you get depressed, and when you get too busy to stay depressed, you go insane. I have more than once been seen chasing floating albino whales through the Baylor parking lots during the wee hours of the morning.

But I'm not being negative about this. I know many people who are taking it a lot worse than I am. When college veterans come back to your high school and tell you that it's not easy, this is what they're talking about. It's not that college requires you to complete monstrous Herculean tasks that sap your strength. They just have you do a bajillion little nitpicky things that drive you mad—hopscotch bunny cup of tea falling wibbly bibbly MAD!

Now, it struck me as odd that I was having to deal with stress because (and anyone who knows me can attest to this) I am one of the most laid-back people I know. Things most people have a hard time taking with a grain of salt, I can usually take with a whole shaker of salt, pepper, and some paprika to boot. I never fretted once over anything grade-wise in high school. I had no late-night panic attacks about tests that I had the next day. To tell the truth, my parents were always more worried about them than I was. So you can imagine how much of a shock it was when I got to college and found that I was actually concerned, and indeed losing sleep, over academic and school-related activities.

I think a lot of it had to do with my writing a book on how to survive college, and in the back of my mind crept a thought. It was: *Wouldn't it be wonderful if you flunked out of college before your book on surviving college hit the shelves?* (I tend to be very sarcastic with myself.) So I started taking my assignments and things seriously. It was only then that I realized what an irreparable mess my organizational system is. On my desk I don't even have stacks of papers. I just have one indiscriminate mound.

So then starts the downward spiral of worry and concern. My usual philosophy, which has served me well, is this: If you can't do anything about it, don't worry about it. This was especially useful in high school when there were many aspects of my life that were beyond my control. However, once again, when I got to college, I found that I was master of my own castle, so to speak. With that freedom, as with all freedom, comes responsibility.

I've always been really good at dealing with freedom, but have a couple of hang-ups when it comes to responsibility. I think you know what I mean. Anyway, the point of this chapter is not to make you panic or anything, but I don't want to say "don't worry about anything" because you, in all reality, actually do need to be somewhat concerned about some things, or you'll become roadkill. However, there are many people I've observed going soooo far toward the opposite extreme—worrying about this and obsessing about that to the

point that it really saps their ability to sit back and have fun.
In my opinion, when you've lost your will or capability for
enjoying life, your life becomes infinitely less worthwhile
than it could or should be.

Ask anyone, college should be a fun time. College is not a time
for getting gray hairs. There's plenty of time for that later. This
is not a call to shirk your responsibilities. It's a call to say "You
know, there's a time for work, but there is also a time to NOT
work." For those of you prone to doing nothing and asking
what the homework assignment was two days after it was due,
this is not for you.

It's just that I'm tired of seeing nineteen and twenty-year-
old people walking around like they've had all the life
sapped out of them. Come on, it's fun when it's fun.
Sure, you have a lot of work to do, but there are many
hours in a day. With some good time management, you
can squeeze at least thirty minutes of fun time during
the most hectic schedule.

So go out and do it! Throw a pie at someone. Have someone
throw one at you, if that's what floats your cheese. In fact, I've
been sitting here writing for too long. I'm going to go do
something fun! Like Sleep! I spell Sleep with a capital "S" now

because I regard it as something like Plato's forms. It's out there somewhere, and it's eternally sought after, but never quite attainable. Anyway, you can see that the late hours are taking their toll on my poor collegiate brain. Goodnight.

Miller Time

It has come to my attention that some people think parties go on at college. It has also come to my attention that my previous sentence was a vast and horribly gross understatement. Just about any time you watch anything about "college" in the movies or on TV, it has something to do with partying, beer, sex, and doing crazy things that one doesn't mention in mixed company. Sometimes it involves all of the above. All in all, most secular colleges are generally thought to be madhouses in which every hour of studying is matched by at least three hours of consumption of illegal substances. At least that's what I thought.

I won't lie to you. Plenty o' drinkin' goes on (said with appropriate Irish flair) around this place. However, there are a few things that don't get portrayed when you're watching the college parties at the movies. First of all, take the panoramic camera angles and bumpin' jumpin' soundtrack out of a college party, and it's really not as exciting as you might think. Sure, crazy things happen at these parties; there's no denying that. But most of them don't compare to the things one can do sober.

You, as a current or prospective college student, are probably very aware of the issues concerning alcohol on college campuses. This, once again, is a point where you find out what kind of person you truly are. If you have a strong moral compass, this is where the rubber meets the road. If, on the other hand, you look forward to escaping your parents' clutches so you can get your sticky hands on some of grandpa's ol' cough medicine, I'm sure you'll be very happy to hear that there is an endless sea of alcohol at your fingertips, just waiting to be consumed.

However, just in case a million better-informed people haven't told you this already, I'm going to let you in on a little secret. Alcohol, if consumed in certain quantities, will affect the work you do. Even though lots of people overlook this, I feel obligated to tell you that here in the collegiate world, if you let the quality of your work slip for a long enough period, they will ask you to leave. When you are asked to leave college, the endless sea of alcohol dries up, and you find yourself in the dry, hot desert, facing your parents. This is a situation that I personally would not look forward to facing. All moral issues aside, alcohol can and will affect your academic performance, if you let it. I have some friends who can attest to that right now.

One thing I learned about college parties both shocked and pleasantly surprised me. This may be the result of going to a private university, but I found that people aren't judgmental if you *don't* drink when attending functions where others *are* drinking. I thought any function that involved alcohol would include a couple of big frat guys walking around the party with a keg on wheels making sure everyone who was there was getting nice and toasty. And if they found anyone whom they thought too sober, they would start pumping alcohol into him by force until he was as drunk as everybody else.

Fortunately for those of us who have no great desire to spend the next morning inspecting porcelain, that is not the case. Those who drink do so, and those who don't, do not do so. The general position among those that drink is, "Hey, that's fine. More for me." The general position among those who don't drink is, "Why in Shakespeare's name would you want to drink mass amounts of something that tastes like carbonated sewage?" At least, that's my thought. So the drinkers and the non-drinkers shall coexist in harmony. Of course, this could just be due to the fact that I go to a Baptist university, and there are more people present with principles than in other places—but I doubt it.

Drinking in college, of course, opens up a plethora of moral issues that I think get overlooked a lot of the time. First and foremost: No matter what you say, and what points you make, if you are not twenty-one and you are consuming alcohol, you are breaking the law. I hate to seem the heavy, but that's a fact most kids disregard simply because everybody else is doing it. It is true that you could easily drink yourself into oblivion every weekend from the day you get to college until the day you turn twenty-one and never suffer any legal repercussions. However, if you consider yourself to be an active, practicing Christian, it would be somewhat hypocritical to . . . blah blah blah, you've heard it all before, so I don't feel any need to preach.

Anyway, the whole point of this chapter is just to encourage you to think before you do things you wouldn't do at home. Believe me, I know that there is a big temptation to do whatever, because now you're not under direct supervision. That's human nature. Now that you're master of your own domain, you want to prove to yourself and the world that you're not mummy and daddy's little kid. So you gather up your canisters of gasoline and matches and set your car on fire in the campus parking garage.

Maybe you're not that extreme (at least I hope not!), but you know what I mean. This is why you need to try to figure out who you are and what you want *before* you go off to college. Because if you don't, you might find that you have defaulted into something you didn't really want to be. Believe me—immorality is fun. If it weren't, it wouldn't be nearly as popular as it is. The straight and narrow is definitely the harder path to take, at least in the short run. It doesn't give you the immediate gratification that doing whatever whenever with whomever will. In this thirty-second-commercial world we live in, we start to believe that anything that doesn't grant immediate gratification probably isn't worth doing.

Everything in our culture tells us that this time of youth and beauty and vigor is the only time that counts for anything. So ignore consequences and throw inhibitions and morals to the wind as you strive for as much fun as you can get your hands on. Now I am treading a very fine line here, because I don't want to be preachy. Good luck. Being a fallible nineteen-year-old myself, I make no claim of having more inherent wisdom than you. I have no theological or moral training, other than living with my parents. (Which, considering their fields of study, probably should count for at least a semester of seminary.) I have tried to figure out what I believe is right universally, and that's all I encourage you to do.

This is the great disadvantage of having to write a book. I wish that instead of writing all of this, I could just sit down and have a conversation with you one on one. Unfortunately time and space don't permit, so I have to do my best to connect with everyone despite not knowing where any of you are coming from.

Me oh my, I've gotten off track, and look where my A.D.D. has taken me. I just looked back at the title of this chapter and realized that not only have I gotten off topic, I have taken you readers on a grand tour of the universe. So, anyway, alcohol is bad for you. Don't binge drink. Because binge drinking leads to several bad things, most of which are associated with the loss of judgment that comes with the brain being infested with little alcohol bubbles. This can, and if given enough chances, will cause you to do things you will regret when you become once-again sober, including driving your car into a lake, or throwing up on your friend's couch. You don't want this to be your fate. At least I hope not.

Anyway, I also don't want to come off as saying that drinking is the worst sin you can commit. If some friends of yours pop a can every now and then, they're not necessarily going to hell in a handbasket, they probably just haven't thought it out all the way through. If they have, then there's probably some underlying problem that needs to be addressed. People in general need friends more than they need accusations, so don't go waving this chapter in their faces or anything.

Well, I think I've said my piece for today. If I said anything you don't agree with, please feel free to rip it straight out of the book. If you so desire you can even put gasoline and C-4 on the book and blow it up for all I care. Just make sure you have purchased it beforehand. Otherwise, I'm finding out who you are and coming after you. Goodnight once again.

Transportation

Since the dawn of time, humanity has been trying to get from point A to point B. It is believed that, given our tendencies, once we finally do get to point B, we will decide that point A was in fact an all-around better spot, and we will spend the rest of our lives trying to get back to point A. This constant restlessness has caused humankind to invent many methods of transportation to aid in this pursuit. There have been several breakthroughs technologically that have contributed considerably to this never-ending quest. These range from the invention of running (discovered shortly after the creation of woman), to llamas, to "all-terrain-heavy-armored-nuclear-invincible-battle-hovercraft." Pretty much all of the above are used and visible on college campuses.

The kind of transportation you take to college will, in a large part, depend on the kind of transportation you owned before you left for college. However, I have been asked a few times by people who have cars if they should take them. So, in this chapter, I'll go through and elaborate on what you will or won't need in the way of wheels, or llamas. (P.S. This chapter is only beneficial for those people reading this book BEFORE they go to college, so if you're already at college, just take this opportunity to go back and read one of the earlier chapters that you enjoyed. Thank you.)

Transportation takes many forms.

Little-known fact: Al Gore invented cars.

Let's suppose that you don't have a car. This means that you probably won't get one any time soon because your parents are most likely going to freak out when they see how much education costs these days. This stinks, I know. I have plenty of friends who lament being carless. It especially stinks if you're a guy, because there's always going to be that guy who drives around in his brand-new Eddie Bauer Abercrombie & Fitch

Tommy Hilfiger BMW. And even though he has the intelligence of an oven mitt, guess who all the girls are going to want to ride with? That's right. Biff. Or whatever his name is.

That said, living without a car at college is not as bad as you might think. This is especially true at a college where people stay put on the weekends. On a college campus, at least 80 percent of the activity that involves college students, even the fun activities, takes place within a three- or four-square-mile radius. Half the stuff is not even a problem to walk to. As for the other stuff, with 30,000 of your closest friends all living within shouting distance, you can usually find someone who is going where you want to go at a time that's convenient.

First semester, Rhett (you remember Rhett) and I basically shared a car, especially after I got injured and needed him to drag my busted self around. When you get right down to it, riding with other people is fun. I'm usually less tempted to have a fit of "road rage" when there are other people in the car—usually. However, you need to be careful about asking for rides, because a person asking for rides too much or at the wrong time can be more annoying than a rabid muskrat in the pants. And that, trust me, is really annoying.

So just remember that if you're living on campus, a car isn't a necessity for college. If you can get your hands on one, I definitely recommend it, but your eternal happiness doesn't depend on it. In fact, that would be kind of strange if it did.

(Outside the gates of heaven)

Angel: *(With flaming sword in hand) Whyfore dost thou think thyself worthy of heaven's glory?*

You: *Well . . . let's see . . . I had a car in college.*

Angel: *No kidding? Well, shoot, grab a halo and have a ball.*

You: *Thanks!*

Now, before this conversation gets too serious, let's move on. Let's suppose that in fact you do have a car. In this case, you will be presented with the dilemma of whether or not to take your car to college. The only reasons, really, why you shouldn't are financial. If you take a car, you're going to have to pay for gas, insurance, maintenance, and all that other good stuff. Not to mention that you're going to have to take care of your car. This is an aspect of life that I have no knowledge of. I think I'm doing well when I keep track of my gas cap for three or more consecutive months.

The problem with keeping your car maintained is all those little moving parts in there. As far as I can tell, this is how it goes: You get your car, and all these little moving parts are sitting there in the engine, near the wheels, under your seat, basically all over the place. Now, at first they work like a charm. They all spin and pump and click and whir and do all their little things perfectly, until something happens like, say, your car gets really old, or you smash it into the side of a church.

Then, just like some kind of little moving-parts labor union, they decide that they're not going to work for you anymore. The air conditioner starts going out, and your power steering, and your brakes, and before you know it, your car doesn't want to move at all. Then you have to call a mechanic who tells you that you're schmelding's gone out, and it will cost a year's tuition to fix it.

Still, in my ever-humble opinion, all of this doesn't eliminate the joys of having a car, if you can afford it. It allows you to be spontaneous. For example, one night, my friends and I decided it would be a good idea to drive around the dark streets of Waco and attempt to find the David Koresh compound. Whether or not this was the brightest of ideas is another issue entirely. The point remains that without my car, I wouldn't have been able to go off in search of the site of an infamous showdown. And that would have been a shame.

Those of you who don't have a car, don't be discouraged. There were three other people in my car who didn't have one of their own. They got to go along for the ride to the site of the infamous showdown as well. So there is plenty of fun to be had for those of you who don't have cars. You just have to use those of us who do.

There are, of course, alternate methods of transportation. These include bicycles, Rollerblades, scooters, mopeds, skateboards, llamas, and "all-terrain-heavy-armored-nuclear-invincible-battle-hovercraft." The only one I've had much experience with are the bicycles. The usefulness of these depends mostly on the size of your campus. Baylor is a good-sized campus, so I took my bike to help me get to class. I bought this brand new lock to make sure that nobody would steal it. The bike has not left the rack since the first day I moved here.

In fact, according to my observations, the number of people who use bikes is greatly outnumbered by those who don't. I find that it's just not worth it for a walking trip that takes ten minutes to spend two minutes on each end chaining the bike back up. As for skateboards, unfortunately, the days of Marty McFly are gone. The skateboard has all but died out on today's college campuses. If you want to try to bring it back, be my guest. (While you're at it, try to bring back the word "radical" too. I miss it.)

Something new on the scene, and very effective for getting around campus, are Rollerblades. They fit into a backpack, and some of them can even fit over your shoes. You just slip them on, and if you know how to use them correctly, you can roll circles around people who are just walking.

I've seen people on these in-line skates going just as fast as bikes. The reason that I cannot totally endorse this method of transportation is that they are not Zach-compatible. They require coordination, which God chose to eliminate from my list of attributes during the early formation of my DNA. I don't think they've found the coordination gene yet, but I'm sure when they do, they'll determine that I don't have one. When using Rollerblades, my feet generally go in two different directions, and my face goes in yet another direction, namely down.

So, once again, this is a good time for some forethought. Try to determine how big your campus is. If you see people loading up backpacks and camping gear to hike to their next class, you might want to look into a little moped or something. Not only are they neat and cute, but they're kind of European, so everyone will think you're a really artsy kind of intelligent espresso-drinking person. But if I truly wanted my ride to reflect my personality, I'd be riding around on a tricycle.

Well, by now you probably know where you fall on this whole transportation issue, and there's nothing more pointless than beating a dead horse—except maybe writing about beating a dead horse. I think I'm going to go to bed. Ah, there's nothing like writing a book at 2:00 in the morning when I have a test in six hours.

College Parking Tip

If you ever get a parking ticket, which you will, don't remove the ticket from your vehicle. Campus security will rarely put

one parking ticket on top of another, so
this method gives you a temporary exemption.

Spring Break

Top Five Fun Things to Do on Spring Break

5. Sleep

4. Not study

3. Not get up

2. Sleep

1. Nothing

In Texas, the season of spring is a local folk myth. Some of the old women of the community sit around and tell stories about how once upon a time there was a space between the extreme cold of winter and the suffocating heat of the summer. This era was said to be pleasant, and when you went outside you didn't have the constant fear of either hypothermia or dehydration. They called this fantastical time "spring."

No one here really believes it, though. We know well enough that once the frostbite stops, we must have our sunburn lotion and solar surface clothing ready to go at a moment's notice. One day in March the sun wakes up and says; "Well I think today is the day." He winds up that nuclear fusion and sends millions of scorching ultraviolet rays directly onto the unsuspecting residents of Texas—and it gets hot.

For some reason, someone somewhere decided that we should have a weeklong holiday to celebrate this process. Who am I to complain? Spring Break on a college campus is nothing short of a phenomenon. The week before Spring Break you can feel the tremors coming. Suddenly people's legs come out of hibernation, and so the campus is full of bright shiny white flesh. The number of people holding hands while walking to class quadruples. The words "tan" and "Cancun" start getting tossed around. Most importantly, people start realizing that the semester isn't going to keep going on and on forever. Some people say "Yeah, the work will stop!" Other people say "Stink, I'd better do some work."

I have no idea what you people from Yankee states do about Spring Break (Yankee states being all of those outside of Texas). As far as I know, you're still buried under 7 feet of permafrost, or something. Speaking of which, my dad is in Siberia right now. Siberia—how ridiculous. He's up there preaching to people who live in places where it's too cold to move. Some of these people have never been farther than 6 feet from the place where they were born. Do you know what they eat up there? Boiled reindeer. I'm not kidding. Apparently that's a good meal. A more rudimentary meal would consist of RAW reindeer (that is reindeer that has not been cooked). Let me clarify: meat that has not been prepared at all since it was out in the snow running around. How does reindeer sushi sound for dinner?

So anyhoo, Spring Break, right? What a trip. I hear about all these people going to the French Riviera and skiing in the Alps, so on and so forth. Well, my adventurous spirit and I are going straight home. I have decided to take Rhett (you remember Rhett) with me. We will see a show in Houston, hang out at my house and with my friends, and everything will be dandy.

Baylor, you see, has the most annoying Spring Break in the universe. For some odd reason, I guess to segregate themselves from all the secular (evil) universities, Baylor decided that they should have their Spring Break a week earlier than everybody else. Some people view this as a good thing, which, on the surface, it is. You go to the beach, and it's totally empty. You get the beach all to yourself. A few minutes later, however, you realize that you're at the beach and you're all by yourself. Which is really nice for two and one-half minutes, but then gets really boring. So, going home wasn't nearly as fun for me, because none of my friends were on Spring Break. Spencer and Andy, however, go to school about an hour from home, so they come back every weekend. I got to visit with them that first weekend, and we rejoiced greatly.

After the first part of the week, I took Rhett to San Antonio and stayed with his family for a couple of days. It's always interesting to see people with real families interact. I come from a family of three, which, according to Spencer, is not a real family. He says that my parents aren't real parents because they haven't had to deal with multiple siblings in the backseat of the car spitting all over each other, or whatever it is that siblings do. I go over to these people's houses, and they greet their little brother with a nice solid punch in the face. Then they ask me if I ever miss having a brother or sister, and I give them this strange look and say "Why?" They respond, "Well, don't you ever want to have someone around to beat up on?"

(Pause for emphasis.) I think many of the evils of society could be cured if everyone was an only child.

So I stayed with Rhett in San Antonio, and I watched more movies per day than I think I ever have before. We hung out and played guitar and went down to the Riverwalk (a downtown commercial and tourist area along the river), and everything was hunky-dory. The sun shown upon us, the birds were singing in the trees, and the entire neighborhood came out of doors to join us for an inexplicably, perfectly choreographed chorus of "Zippity-Do-Dah." These things happen on Spring Break.

Then, as suddenly as it came, it was time to leave San Antonio, choreography and all. So I took the long road home, and there was silence at last. Silence, during college life, is an oddity. Your roommates are running in and out, and even when they're not, you have a civil war going on in the hallway. Then you go out of your room and there are 10,000,000 people going this way and that, and even your private moments to yourself include a dozen people watching you. It was out of this context that I arrived home to my house containing only myself and my parents (who were gone half the time). I found myself sitting around with silence anxiety. Right now, for example, with no sound but the wind blowing by the house, I'm sitting in my room thinking, *This is not right. Something needs to be happening.*

Spencer and Andy were not due back until the weekend, and my only friend who stayed in town after high school works like a mad fiend during the week. So I was left to myself with many hours in which I had nothing to do. I had brought neither my computer nor my guitar with me from school, and there I was, staring at an empty house. I finally realized just how low I had sunk and how bored I had become when I unloaded the dishwasher for fun. I had never thought of myself as the kind of person who unloads dishwashers for fun.

I took the only option that I saw available to me. Please don't think me less of a person for this, but I went back to my high school—just to visit. This contradicts about half the things I said during my senior year at this school. "When I get out of here, I'm never looking back," and so on. And here, less than a year later, I found myself sitting in a high school classroom with people I had once ruled over, saying, "Hey guys, what's going on?" Life's irony is cruel.

Of course, it's not all that bad. I have several good friends who are still in high school. It was just very odd walking in the front door and thinking, *I have no obligation to be here. I could very easily walk out of here without any negative repercussions. Oh well.* I had an enjoyable day walking down memory lane. One thing I noticed: It's amazing how extraordinarily well your high school gets along without you. Instead of calling all classes to a halt and holding a pep rally in my honor, I was greeted with a "Hey." Some people said they missed me, but that was it. Lesson learned: You are not quite as important as you might think you are.

So the week ended, and the rest of my friends came down from their collegiate perch, and we had some fleeting moments of camaraderie, and basically spent our time laughing together. I noticed that although I was enjoying my second semester immensely, I hadn't been laughing nearly as much as I should have been. Having a good time simply isn't worth it if you don't bust a gut while you're doing it.

The real key to laughter is finding genuinely funny people. This goes back to that whole important issue of finding friends. Going back home showed me just how much I still need to work on relationships at college if I really want to enjoy myself. After all, what good is the funniest joke in the world if you have no one to listen to it?

As soon as it came, Spring Break was over, and we wayward students filed back onto campus. Then we got to turn on the TV and watch everyone else who was on Spring Break. Spring Break, according to TV, is very different than what I experienced. For one thing, everybody had on a lot less clothing. For another thing, everyone seemed to be able to dance. Dancing is non-existent to me. I move like a 6'3" white boy trained from youth to play basketball—because that's what I am.

Anyway, go off, have fun, bask in the sunlight, go crazy, knock yourself out. Just remember that finals lurk in the near future, and with them the promise of summer! For ideas on how to better spend your Spring Break, call the Zach Arrington Spring Break Fun Fund at 1-800-SUN-FUNN.

Fraternizing and All Things Greek

The author has mixed feelings on the subject he is about to present. In fact, the author still doesn't entirely know what his position is on the matter. Before coming to a university, my thoughts on fraternities, sororities, and the Greekier parts of college society were somewhat different than they are now. I thought, *Why on earth would you want to pay exorbitant fees to join what basically amounts to a party club? You shouldn't have to buy your friends.* The notion of social politics has always made me somewhat nauseated—and still does.

So here I come to college, diametrically opposed to anything Greek, and thinking that the people who take part in them just needed a social crutch. Of course, God puts me in a room with a guy who is chomping at the bit to rush a fraternity.

Maybe at this point I should stop and explain how, to the best of my knowledge the Greek system works (I don't think anyone really knows for sure). First, you go to college. That in itself is a pretty big step. For more information on that see chapters 1 through 3, and pretty much the rest of the book.

Next you have to set your eye on a particular Greek organization. There may be several options open to you. For instance, here at Baylor, there are 7.5 million Greek clubs available for you to rush. That doesn't even count the independent student organizations. All these Greek clubs have names like "Alpha Delta Zeta" or "Nu Nu Nu." They always use Greek letters for names; thus they are called Greek organizations. The letters apparently stand for something "secret" that you are told when you get initiated. It's like a box of Cracker Jacks. As far as I can tell, the people in charge just pick them at random, plaster them on thousands of shirts, and off they go.

Something I didn't know before going to college is that fraternities come in all shapes and sizes. I shall now refer to all Greek organizations (yes, that includes sororities) as fraternities, because I am a guy, and all guys intrinsically care only about themselves and the things that apply to them.

Oh, and for those of you who are currently foaming at the mouth because you haven't heard about any of this before, fraternities are strictly for guys and sororities are solely for girls. There are no exceptions. I checked.

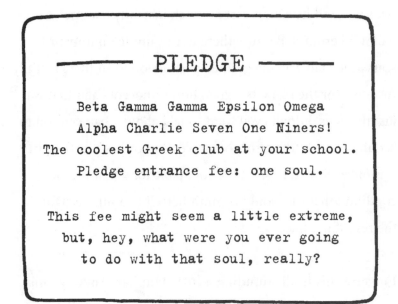

— **PLEDGE** —

Beta Gamma Gamma Epsilon Omega
Alpha Charlie Seven One Niners!
The coolest Greek club at your school.
Pledge entrance fee: one soul.

This fee might seem a little extreme,
but, hey, what were you ever going
to do with that soul, really?

Anyway, I have noticed that fraternities bear an uncanny resemblance to the "table system" that was used in elementary school. For those of you who don't remember the "table system," or have blocked it out of your memory, I'll recap it for you. Remember Bobby Awesome? He was the kid on the cutting edge of fourth-grade society. He had the Reebok Pump shoes before anybody else. He was the first kid you saw playing with a Teenage Mutant Ninja Turtle. He was "it." There is one of him at every school.

He would usually have a second in command, a lieutenant, so to speak. This was someone with whom he would share his treasure of trendiness and play Ninja Turtles. Wherever this twosome and its cohorts sat at lunch instantly became hallowed ground. Because there were a limited number of seats at the table, being granted permission to sit there by Billy Awesome or the like was a great honor indeed—and that was just the boys. I don't even want to talk about what went on to acquire a seat at the girls' cool table. Rumor has it that a girl was once allowed to sit at the cool table for a year on the condition that she would commit herself to a nunnery for the rest of her life.

I'm sure this is all sounding a little familiar. Anyway, this all goes to support my theory that you are never more mature than the second semester of your junior year of high school. You get to high school and start thinking, *Gosh, I'm in the big leagues, I'd better start acting it up.* So you add maturity to your list of virtues and start growing up. Then during the first semester of your senior year, you realize what a joke it's all been, and take a running leap back to where you left off in eighth grade. The next year, as a freshman in college you decide that junior high is too sophisticated, jump straight back to kindergarten, and look for the nearest sandbox.

The point is, just as you had your "cool table," your "second-string cool table," your "loser table," and your "people who are too weird to fit in any other category table," you have your fraternities that occupy different niches along the social spectrum. You have your "good Christian boy" fraternities all the way to your "commit a felony and you're in" fraternities. And they all think they are the greatest single institution ever to be blessed with existence. They churn out T-shirts by the thousands. They have "events."

These events are what get your foot in the door, if you want to rush. (I know I haven't explained what "rushing" is, but all will become clear in time.) These events start just about the second you set foot on campus. This is where the process of getting into a fraternity starts to bug me. You have to go to these events, and I guess the existing fraternity brothers take roll, or something, because they take note of who's there. Those who come to events get social points toward making it as a fraternity brother. The process of making the "right" friends has officially begun.

The rushing process is basically this: You decide what fraternity you'd like to be a part of, you declare that publicly, and you do everything you can to kiss the shoes of those who are already in the fraternity. Getting into a fraternity is basically like trying out for a sports team. You find yourself competing against several of your fellow classmates for a limited number of spots. In this case if you're rejected, it's not on the basis of your athletic skills, but on how "cool" you are. I'm sure you can see that it still bugs me. So you try out, they decide if they like you, and then invite you to pledge.

Pledging means that you are committed to a certain fraternity. Then they take you and proceed to treat you like the scum of the earth. This includes your doing absolutely everything that the fraternity brothers tell you to do. If that means cleaning every surface of the frat house with a toothbrush, this is your fate. Generally, when you are pledging, you don't have time to do anything else. It is by the good graces of the fraternity brothers alone if you get home before 2:00 A.M. A good friend of mine failed two-thirds of his classes because of pledging. It is not for the weak of heart.

This process goes on for awhile, and right at the point when you think you're going to lose all semblance of sanity they say "Okay, you're cool. You're a member now." They initiate you, and then it's all parties and celebration and hooray. I have no idea what goes on after that point. Once you're initiated though, you are never again hassled like when you were a pledge. You're a member. You've arrived. As long as you pay your dues, you're in. There are some students who drop out and become inactive members after a couple of years, and there are those who go to every activity they are physically able to attend throughout their college career.

There really are two sides to this issue. I have always been of the philosophy "Let your friends be friends, let your enemies be enemies, and don't lobby to get either of them." Social politics, as I said before, make me nauseated. This is the main reason that before coming to college I was so against the idea of fraternities. I just had this flashback from my childhood of a bunch of kids sitting in a treehouse and saying, "Nyah, nyah! You can't come up here. It's a secret club!"

Well, coming here and actually seeing the beast in action has given me a different perspective. There is indeed some nanny nanny boo-booing that goes on, but for many people, Greek clubs are vital to the survival of their college social life.

The reason for a fraternity's importance? Well, when you were in high school, you had maybe a couple thousand people in the entire school. If your school was on the obscenely huge end, you might have seven or eight thousand, but those are the exceptions. If you have just a couple thousand people (or less) in your school, as I did, then the chances are good that you can get to know almost everyone in your class, and the surrounding classes, by the time you graduate.

Chances are you also had some area of specialty, such as athletics or band or art—take your pick. These extracurricular clubs gave you a peer group to identify with. This gave you an automatic "home," so to speak. A lot of your friends probably came from these groups, and it gave you an anchor. At college there are no such given anchors. You suddenly find yourself floating amidst a mass of people you don't know—and who don't know you—and in their ignorance don't really care if they know you.

I found a loophole in this cycle because of my theater major. There are only about 100 theater majors at Baylor, and we all spend our waking hours at the theater. This allows us to get to know each other pretty well. Right now, all, and I mean ALL, of my friends are theater majors. I find myself with no way to communicate to the outside world because I don't know if I have anything in common with them.

So, those people who are business majors, which is about 60 percent of the school, could get totally lost. That's where the fraternities come in handy. If you make it in, you automatically have a peer group, conveniently sized so you can get to know everyone in it with relative ease.

But here's the real advantage of the Greek system: Fraternities get together and socialize with sororities. It is virtually impossible, save by divine intervention, for me to meet new women. There's always the "go up to them at random during lunchtime at the cafeteria," but who does that, really? It's not the way to go.

Undeniably, there are pros and cons about this system. The way I see it now, it's kind of like our democratic system of government. Sure it's far from perfect, and sometimes we may despise the parties involved, but it's the best thing we've come up with so far—and it works. Kind of. So, love it or leave it, you're going to have to deal with the Greek system. Unless you go my route and start singing "Hi diddly dee, an actor's life for me."

The Great Apartment Safari

As great as the dorms are, and believe me they are great, there comes a point in your life when you say, "The time has come to move on to something bigger and better." For me that point was as soon as possible/immediately/now. The dorms started off being "neat." It was a new experience that was fresh and exciting, I was finally away from home, and wow! It took me about half a semester to realize that I had gotten myself into sharing, along with two other guys, a room that was scarcely three-fourths the size of my own room at home. Parents or no parents, that's going to be annoying.

Thus, during my second semester at Baylor University, I, the young and valiant Sir Zach, set upon finding myself a new dwelling place. The task was not easy. Trying to determine the best place to abide for an entire year while dealing with financial constraints could have easily proved to be a daunting task.

If you wish to follow in Sir Zach's footsteps, you must first determine your price range. If your father happens to be Bill

Gates, then you probably won't have to worry about this aspect of the apartment hunting process. However, for those of us with middle-class means, money is a real issue. As for my family, we couldn't possibly afford to shell out one cent more than we were already shelling out. Indeed, we didn't know how much longer we could continue to maintain the current level of shelling out.

So, as a novice "apartment hunter," probably the best action to take is to ask around for those who have already gone through this experience. Seek out upperclassmen, for example. This exercise helps in just about all aspects of college life. In fact, that's the very reason I'm writing this book: To give insider help from someone who's been there. Having been there and survived gives one valuable advice to dispense. You can probably find someone with experience in whatever it is you must accomplish.

Fortunately for me, I didn't have to go out on a grand adventure to find an apartment and roommates. They came looking for me. Erik, a friend of mine from the theater department, was looking for someone to room with him and Chris, another mutual friend. Apparently they were looking for a raving lunatic to room with, because they came to me and asked if I wanted to go in with them on an apartment.

This apartment was Erik's sister's, who was a senior, and as such wouldn't be needing it next year. This whole string of coincidences made getting my apartment about 150,000 times easier than it should have been.

The usual process involves contacting the people who own or manage the building, being dictated your rent, and then being dictated what kinds of things you can do in your apartment. The whole apartment thing is very totalitarian.

To me, the fun part about renting an apartment is the contracts. You are given these ridiculously long pieces of paper with many stipulations on them. They read something like this:

```
Wherefore and hereupon the undersigned
potential occupant hereby releases all claim
on said soul to the underwriters thereupon
mentioned, unless thereupon mentioned
underwriters deem the undersigned potential
occupant in direct, indirect, or
subdirectionalized violation of anything
the thereupon mentioned underwriters please.
Furthermore, the undersigned shall, and by
signing agrees that (he) (she) (it) shall
```

never perform otherwise, and stand on (his)
(her) (its) head in a corner until the
thereupon mentioned underwriters are amused.
Henceforthwith is a list of actions that
the undersigned potential occupant shall
never, under peril of eternal unpleasantness,
take part in:

1) The undersigned potential occupant will
   never make, or by absence of action cause
   to be made, any holes, dents, scratches, or
   aesthetic changes that are not cleared with
   the thereupon mentioned underwriters. Nor
   shall they take part in any activity that
   may lead to said changes. This includes
   leaning up against a wall harshly.

2) The undersigned potential occupant shall
   not bring any pets into the apartment. This
   includes dogs, cats, snakes, birds, rats,
   marmots, bears, mammoths, sharks, cloned
   dinosaurs, or unusually large bacteria.

3) The undersigned potential occupant may not
   engage in behavior that disturbs other

undersigned occupants. You must keep your
radios turned down and your domestic
fights quiet.

4) The undersigned potential occupant must
surrender his/her soul at the end of the
tenancy. There can be no discussion on
this point. It's just the way we do things
around here.

Sure, there may be a lot of rules and regulations about living in an apartment, but at least you can stretch without poking your roommate in the eye. Also, for those of us at Baylor, getting an apartment is of the utmost importance because it allows you to have members of the opposite sex visit you at times other than 1:00-6:00 on Saturdays and Sundays.

Do you know sometimes when you get a thought in your head and it's really funny, but you don't know how to express it? I had one of those when I wrote the title for this chapter. "Apartment Safari." I have this vision of that Australian crocodile hunter guy standing outside an apartment complex and saying, "These apartments are *really* dangerous. In fact, these are the most dangerous apartments I've ever seen.

Don't get too close to them, because they get really angry.
I'm going to stick my head in them . . . etc. etc."

Well, I wish you good luck and good riddance to dorm life
as your search for your own little Shangri La ensues.

Chapter
Twenty-Seven

Dating (Chaperones Not Included)

Writing this chapter scares the walrus out of me. I first had the idea back when I put the proposal together for this book at the end of my high school senior year. Today is Friday and finals start next Wednesday. My freshman year is almost over. This chapter has been a long time in coming. Rather, I should say, it has been delayed a long time. The reason it has been delayed so long is that I feel totally and completely inadequate to write a chapter on dating, especially giving others advice on dating.

It's not that I have no experience in this area. It's just that I don't think I've really gotten it right yet. In fact, given that I'm "single" right now, I'm quite sure I haven't gotten it right. So for this chapter, don't just take the usual disclaimer of "I may be incorrect;" instead take this disclaimer: "I am most likely cross-eyed blitheringly out and out wrong, so feel free to laugh at me."

Instead of trying to write about dating itself, I'm going to focus on the difference between dating in high school and dating in college. Plenty of dating books have been written by people who have their Ph.D. in dating. The purpose of these books, it seems, is to get everybody paranoid and confused about which planet they're from (Mars or Venus, Venus or Mars?). Since mine is just a book about college, I'll stick to what I know.

What I know is that I have dated girls in high school, and I have dated a couple of girls in college. I haven't had any really serious girlfriends in college. A couple of times I have thought about walking up to some random girl and saying, "Hi, my name is Zach, and I'm writing a book. I need to do some research on dating. Could you do me a favor and go out with me for a couple of months?" Although pretty unconventional, I think that makes for a pretty good pick-up line. Unfortunately all of my test subjects gave it two thumbs down.

Aside from that, here is a comprehensive list of the things I know about interaction between the sexes: First off (and guys you might want to write this down), there are three facts that I know for sure about women. 1) They are not men. This statement alone covers most of the unique characteristics about women, such as their ability to bear children and pick out wallpaper. 2) They are better. I'm not really sure that I totally agree with this statement, but guys, if you say it often and loudly enough, you might find that your life gets easier. Finally, 3) The only surefire way to get their attention is to buy them something they know you can't afford. Many women I've talked to disagree with this, but deep down they all know a guy who buys them a diamond has a much better chance than a guy who picks them a flower.

Now, if you're like most people, this act of dating probably started when A) You started becoming attracted to members of the opposite sex, and B) Your parents allowed you to start dating. Technically, I don't think I was allowed to "single date" until I moved out of my parents' house. However, I had my share of girlfriends, they came over, and we went out and did things. My parents knew about all of them, so I think that constitutes "dating."

For many people, dating constitutes going out to do something fun with a particular member of the opposite sex more than one time. Hence, Bill and Jane went to the movies together twice within the last month. They are now dating. This type of dating can supposedly be done non-exclusively without anyone's feelings getting hurt. I have yet to see that proven.

Then there's the more conventional idea of dating, which states that two people who are interested in each other must, according to the laws of "young love," bind themselves to each other for a certain length of time, acting as if there is no one else in the universe. When the allotted time is up, or when one member of the pair realizes that there are, in fact, other people in the universe, they abruptly part ways, causing themselves and their counterparts much anguish.

I'm sure you've seen this pattern repeated again and again, and if you're really lucky, have taken part in it a few times yourself. There have been a few attempts by Christians to help these unfortunate people break free from this pattern—Joshua Harris' *I Kissed Dating Goodbye*, for example. I think that these new ideas are all fine and good. Whatever floats your boat. It's just that this is America, and as long as hot dogs are sold on the earth, people are going to have good old-fashioned dysfunctional dating relationships.

I'm not here to beat the drum about whether to date or not to date, or how you should date. I'm writing a book about college, and this chapter is (or should be) about how dating pertains specifically to college.

On today's college campus, the process usually goes something like this: Guy meets Girl. Guy and Girl get interested in each other. Guy and Girl express this to each other. Guy and Girl become a Couple. The Couple becomes more and more wrapped up in itself and starts to ignore anyone on the outside, namely friends. The Couple decide that they are in love and no one in the world could possibly be more in love than they are.

The way I look at it, there are only two ways a relationship can end—death or breaking up. That might be a pretty morbid way of looking at it, but it's the truth. If you don't get married, you HAVE to break off at some point or another. Eventually, in our story about the Couple, somebody gets the idea into his or her head to break up. After that, everything goes downhill. Once the notion to break up has been firmly planted, be it by boredom, exhaustion, or active interest in someone else, it cannot be prevented—only delayed.

Once the dreaded breakup does occur, both parties of the Couple find themselves devastated. If the Couple was not paying attention to the fact that the only two ways a relationship can end are by death or breaking up, they may have made the unfortunate decision to have sex. They have then given up everything to each other, and often find they have alienated themselves from their former friends. Nobody wins. The only way that sex really works is in the context of a relationship that is fueled by love and lasts forever. Otherwise it just messes with your mind, making promises that cannot be kept.

You see, Christianity is really a practical religion. Its tenets and teachings solve real problems and make sense in the real world. The moral limitations that Christianity places on us, which some people may view as constrictive, are all there for our own protection. That, to me, is one of the greatest arguments for the truth of Christianity. It addresses genuine human needs. It, in short, works.

Taking all of that into consideration and setting it aside, dating should be fun. It's not something you should be stressing out about. Shoot, you're still young. One time my grandfather, whom I consider to be a very wise individual, said, "Life is too short to ever take anything seriously." (This, of course, from a man who risked his life in the Pacific in WWII and boot-strapped his own business.) I don't know if his words are something to build a life philosophy on, but it's something to think about. Obviously you need to be thinking ahead to life and the future, but what's the point if you never really enjoy it?

The point I'm really trying to make here is that I see so many couples who get so involved in each other that everything becomes too serious. Their entire world gets wrapped around this other person and it becomes like a mini-marriage. Scrap that attitude. Just go out and have fun with people. Have fun with girls (or if you are a girl—guys). If you happen to become romantically attached to one of them, have fun with that, too. Do random, creative, fun things. Have a picnic. Set up a lemonade stand. Go to the bank and tell them you're getting married. (Don't ask, it's a long story.)

By now you've probably been able to discern that a large part of my life philosophy goes something like, "You're full of youth. Take advantage of it." I don't know what I'm going to do when I have outgrown this. What will I do when I'm forty? Probably change it to something like, "You're old and wise. Take advantage of it."

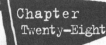

The Last Hurrah

It has come at last. There were several times when I doubted I would survive to see it, but I did. I have fought the good fight, run the long race, and beat the bad marmot to death. It is the end of the year. People, one by one like little tributaries, are trickling out of this place of higher education, going back to their particular places of origin. Watching them leave, I suddenly realize that I am going to miss them. For the past several months, I have eaten, breathed, and studied with these people, and I have become so wrapped up in everything that I hadn't been able to realize how much I genuinely liked them.

My room is empty now. One of my roommates has gone, taking the television with him. I sit and stare at the window. All of the silly little posters and pictures that used to adorn the walls are now packed away, leaving the walls barren. I can't help but think back to the first time that I saw this room. The first word that came to my mind when I saw it was "lawnmower." I don't really understand that, but that's just the way my mind works. The second, and more applicable word that came into my head was "cell." In a matter of months, the word "cell" had been replaced with "home" without any conscious thought.

The most turbulent year of my life has come and gone, and I haven't had time to notice. New things were thrust upon me with such swiftness and immediacy that the only thing I could do was accept them. Looking at the person I used to be and the person I have become makes me realize, beyond a doubt, that this year has changed me fundamentally. I'll be quite honest. Some of these changes I do not like. In some small ways, I have grown up. That makes me nauseated. I have never wanted to grow up. Survival has forced upon me the habits of responsibility, organization, and (gag) social graces.

The strength of the human species is to adapt; to survive. Those who are not up to the task of adapting are weeded out. I ought to laugh at myself here. I don't want to make it seem like college is going to take you in, make you into some corporate clone, and spit you back out. It will put you through the fire. It will test what you are made of. It will refine you, not destroy you.

I studied for all my finals in a daze. I was in "finish the race" mode. I went workaholic for a week and made sure I did everything right so I wouldn't have to go back and do it again. I laughed and talked and consorted with my friends, but all the while I was in the same state of mind that one has immediately after a car accident. All of a sudden you're safe and standing on the curb looking at your wrecked car and thinking, "OK, what just happened here? I can't believe I just . . . etc."

I took stock of those I now consider close friends. Just months before, they had been total strangers. It's humbling to realize just how much our lives are shaped by "chance." (By "chance" I mean this infinitely intricate and unknowable will of God that we're all walking around in.)

We all gathered at Common Grounds, the local coffeehouse, to laugh and hug and say our good-byes. It wasn't a tearful occasion. We are just taking a really long weekend. We'll see everyone on the flip side and have plenty of time to get sick of one another again. There were so many faces. I marveled at how close I had grown to these people without ever realizing it.

Friends are a funny thing. It's not nearly as simple as it used to be to get them. Back in the day (kindergarten—where else?), if you wanted someone to be your best friend, you just asked, "Will you be my best friend?" You may have even offered your very best friendship in exchange for some kind of service, like being given the extra Twix stick.

Through four years of high school, a small group of very close friends were the pillar of my existence. By some strange twist of the crazy will of God, I found myself separated from them. I think my initial separation shock at the beginning of college cast a big dark cloud over the rest of the year. I felt so alienated. I was always second-guessing myself, which is not something I'm good at. That caused all kinds of negative repercussions.

The moral of the story is that if you can be yourself, and avoid worrying about fitting in and impressing people, you will find people who like you—and whom you like. I had spent so much time lamenting the fact that I didn't have any friends when they were there staring me right in the face the entire time.

Anyway, right now the campus is filled with parents who have come to help their kids move back home for the summer. College leads to a drastic perspective change with your parents. Instead of simply being the kinsmen that have been lording it over you your entire life, they become people. You begin to realize they have real emotions, rational reasons for doing things, and can even be funny at times—though not too often. (Ha ha, just kidding, *Dad.*)

I know your mom may have gone a little batty when you were preparing to leave, and she may get a little overeager for your return, but other than that, parents become pretty cool. You start to realize what spectacular people they really must be to have put up with you for all your life. If you look closely enough, you just might catch a glimpse of what you will become in a few years.

I decided to give myself an extra day to pack instead of trying to get everything ready and rush home immediately. Plus, several of my friends were staying, and we decided to rent a movie. We felt like having a good laugh that night. Instead of renting a comedy, however, we did what may be the most fun thing you can do at a video store. We went through that entire mountain of tapes, looking for the absolute worst movie we could find. What we came up with was an intended psychological thriller, but it wound up making us laugh wholeheartedly.

That horrible, forgettable, stupid movie was the perfect way to leave. While watching it we had fun together. No matter how much I grow up, I never intend to lose the ability to have fun. All the riches, wisdom, morals, education, and achievements

in the world do you no good if you don't enjoy it in the end—
or in the process.

It seems that a lot of people think "becoming an adult" means
you must set aside enjoyment of life and instead focus on
success. Whether it's financial success or domestic success,
you're supposed to be relentless in your climb to the top, at the
expense of fun. I think that's a crime. I'm sure Jesus laughed
a lot more than He cried. That's just not what we read about.

The world is full of excitement. Life abounds with joy and
music and beauty. The fact that people can overlook it stuns
me. Seize every opportunity to laugh and to make others
laugh. If you just look at the world around you with a fresh
pair of eyes, you can't help but smile. There's so much hope
and laughter to be realized out there. It's sitting out there right
under the world's nose. Hardly anyone recognizes it, even
though the world needs it so desperately. At the risk of
sounding like a hopeless optimist (which I am), spread
the light and pass the salt.

✳✳✳✳✳

I load everything into my car, filling every available square
inch of space. The two open square inches I started out with

on the trip up here have now shrunk to a quarter of an inch because of the stuff I have bought this year. I run up to the front desk and sign out, returning my key, and swing by my room for one last check before I head back home.

I go over the room one last time for anything I may have left behind. All the nooks, crannies, and corners have been cleaned out meticulously. It gives me sort of a shock when I realize that I am the one who did the cleaning. I never knew I was capable of this much organization. Everything looks to be in place. I give the mirror one last sweep, sprinkle the holy water and declare, "This room is clean!"

I walk out of the room, pretending that I'm not ever going to look back. I get about 3 feet. The door hasn't even shut before I decided I must go back and have a last silent moment with the pathetic little box that has been my home. As I open the door, I am amazed at how untouched the room looks. Every trace of our existence has been removed. The chairs are face down on the desks, just as we were instructed to put them.

The bare walls gleam white; nothing of the personality we hung on them remains.

I cannot help but think back to the first time I walked in this door and had this view. I was carrying an armful of stuff and preparing to start out on a new phase of my life. The sun of the afternoon bounced off the floor and spread around the room, illuminating it.

I remark to myself how very much like that first entrance this room looks now. I also realize how different I feel now. The person who first entered this room is not the same one now leaving it. The room has not changed. The occupant has.

Epilogue

Well, that's it. It's done. Not only am I finished with an entire year of college, but also a book too. I hope you enjoyed the book as much as I enjoyed the year of college. I hope it hasn't taken you quite that long to read. It has been an interesting process, writing down what I think about everything. It's a process of self-discovery, I'll tell you. In order to write down what you think about things, you must first make sure you know exactly what you think.

As a teenager, this is not always easy. This is the time in life when I'm just beginning to realize that all life's answers aren't going to be handed to me on a silver platter. They have to be figured out by a grueling process of real-life trial and error. That was my motivation for writing this book. I had no idea what I would face at college, and I wanted to try and answer some of the same questions I had asked for the benefit of those coming behind me. I hope I have done this, and if not, at least I hope you are not thoroughly confused.

If you are confused...don't worry. I still have no idea what the future holds for me. I now have a band, tentatively called

"Flyrail." We're tentatively called Flyrail because three of us are from the theater department, and have had to operate a stage flyrail and we can't think of anything else. There's a little Zach trivia for you.

Anyway, we're pretty good, I think. We just might do something. Then there's this whole book thing. Of course, there's my field of study—acting—which some say is just majoring in waiting tables.

The point is, don't get discouraged if you don't know what's in store for your life. Although we take an active part in our lives, we're all basically just along for the ride. Don't stress out about it. I don't. I trust that God knows what He's doing, and even if He didn't there wouldn't be a lot I could do about it. Just work your hardest and see what gets accomplished.

This is the last chapter I get to write for this book. It's kind of sad. I don't want to let go. I think I might just write down everything I think from now on, just for fun. Wow, that would be really weird. Right. Well, it's been a pleasure. I hope this book has been more fun than, say, a driver's ed handbook.

I'm trying to think of a good way to end all this. Staying true to form, it should be something funny and completely random. Ah, here we go:

So this guy walks into a bar, right? He strolls on up to the bar and asks the bartender for a drink. The bartender looks at him. The guy looks a little down on his luck, unshaven, kind of dirty. "How you gonna pay?" the bartender asks. The guy fishes in his wallet, finds that he has nothing—but comes up with an idea. He says, "Look, I haven't any money, but what if I showed you something you've never seen before? Would you let me have the drink?" The bartender says, "All right, show me what you've got."

The guy reaches in his coat and takes out an Alaskan marmot and sets it down on the bar. It immediately runs down the bar, jumps on the piano and starts playing the most beautiful rendition of Mozart that the bartender has ever heard. He says, "Wow, that's some trick! That's certainly worth a drink." So the guy downs his drink and says, "How about another one?" The bartender looks at him and says, "Sorry, but you need another miracle for another drink."

Out of the other side of his coat, the guy pulls this turtle. He sets the turtle down and it sticks out its head and starts singing this glorious opera music. Some guy from the back of the bar stands up and says, "That's incredible! I'll give you $300 for that turtle right now!" The guy says, "Sure," takes the money and hands him the turtle.

While pouring the drink the bartender says, "Man, that turtle was amazing. You could have made a lot more than $300 off that." The guy looks up and says, "What, the turtle? Nah. That was just the marmot throwing its voice."

Appendix A

Note to Reader:

Author's Opinion on Appendices. Webster defines an appendix as "a blind branch of the intestine." Now, why it is customary for books to have these in order to supplement material is beyond me. I guess it's one of those things like the "ph" making an "f" sound. You don't question it. It's just there. That said, this is the appendix referenced in chapter 1. If, for some reason, chapter 1 had caused you to go into convulsions and experience severe distress, you are advised to rip out this section of the book as quickly as possible.

Unlike biological appendices, this one actually has a purpose. While the narrative of chapter 1 is designed for your reading pleasure, this appendix is here for reference and to give you tips that you may or may not find helpful. These are just mental notes I made for myself when preparing to move off to college. I hope you live a happier life as a result of them.

Before You Pack
(BYP, if you like acronyms)

These are some things I didn't necessarily do, but I kind of wish I had. If you're anything like me, you have stashed away, in your room, items you haven't touched since you were eleven. But somehow you don't feel you can throw them away. Here's what you can do.

Make a list! List everything you want to take with you to college. Just take into consideration that you're only going to be able to store about 20 percent of it when you get there.

Prioritize everything you own. Sure, there are a lot of things that you like, but take only the things you're really going to USE. Functionality is the key here. You know what? Functionality is a silly word. You have to work in an office to use that word. Just take the things you are actually going to use.

Buy a hanging rod. Don't try to fold all of your clothes and take them to college. You will wind up with a bunch of wrinkled clothes. I was fortunate enough to get a hanging rod, and the only clothes I could wear with dignity the first week were those that were hung on that rod.

Now Pack! And Be Quick About It!

There. Now that you have loaded the car, you are ready to go to college. Before stepping into the vehicle, take a good look around. Sniff the warm summer air (if you live below the Arctic Circle). Hear the birds chirping. Smell the roses. This will be the last time that life is going to be this tranquil for awhile.

Once You Arrive
(You are finally at college! Now the real fun starts.)

Most likely, the first sight you will see when you arrive on campus are hundreds of other people, with just as much stuff as you have, trying to crowd through the same door you are. This is your first "college line." Enjoy it. There will be many more to come.

Mark Your Territory! Once in your room, it is very important to decide which space is going to be yours. You must defend this territory; otherwise it will become someone else's.

Organize! Organize! Organize! I hate the sound of that word. It makes my skin crawl. It's like the smell of fresh-cut grass. I hate it. But it is a necessary component of the moving-in process. Remember that tomorrow you're going to need to know where to find all this stuff, and you don't want to go a-rummaging.

Prioritize Again! You will use some things more than other things. Make sure that these things are readily accessible. For instance: Do not place your toothbrush and bathroom supplies underneath your laundry hamper. This may seem like common sense, but you'd be surprised at the kind of things you can do while trying to unpack in a hurry.

Now you are done unpacking. You have successfully moved into a room the size of a cardboard box. Congratulations. Now I would recommend sleeping. Enjoy.

Appendix B
A Final Note on Baylor University

In the process of writing this book I may have critiqued various and sundry characteristics of Baylor University here and there, but that's simply because it's where my life is taking place and we all complain about our own lives. It was not my intention to malign this distinguished university. Baylor is a great place, a great school. The excellent academics, beautiful campus, and really interesting people (like me) make it a great place to attend college. Yeah, Baylor!

About the Author

Zach Arrington, who penned this book during his freshman year at Baylor University in Waco, Texas, is currently completing his Bachelor of Fine Arts Degree in Theater Performance. (Some call this majoring in waiting tables.) He has already appeared in several productions, including a role in the classic comedy, *How To Succeed in Business Without Really Trying.*

A native of Tomball, Texas (a small town) just outside of Houston, Texas (a really big town), Zach still officially makes his home with his parents, Jack and Lael. Zach copes with the stress of college by playing guitar and piano, writing music, watching a lot of movies, and warning his friends about the dangers of playing on power lines.

Up to this point, Zach has led a typical all-American life. Four years at Tomball High School were primarily spent in the theater department, choir room, and on the basketball court. While quite enjoyable, these idyllic years did little to prepare him for the dangers that lay ahead—like cleaning his own socks.

Now, at the age of 19, Zach has gained a wealth of knowledge and wisdom that he shares in this, his inaugural work. On any given day, Zach can be found sitting around in his apartment procrastinating, listening to music, and discovering the Secret of Life—only to forget where he left it.

Additional copies of this book and other titles
by RiverOak Publishing are available from
your local bookstore.

If you have enjoyed this book,
or if it has impacted your life,
we would like to hear from you.

Please contact us at:

RiverOak Publishing
Department E
P.O. Box 700143
Tulsa, Oklahoma 74170-0143

Or by e-mail at info@riveroakpublishing.com